Responsive Legality

Responsive Legality is an important book about twenty-first-century justice. It explores the legal and moral values that twenty-first-century public officials use to make their decisions, engaging existing theoretical models of administrative justice and updating them to reflect changed twenty-first-century conditions. Together, these features of twenty-first-century public administration are coined 'responsive legality'. Whereas twentieth-century public officials were generally driven by their concern for bureaucratic rationality, professional treatment, moral judgement and – towards the end of the century – the logics of 'new managerialism', the twenty-first-century public official embodies greater complexity in their characteristic pursuit of substantive and procedural justice. In responsive legality, government decision makers show a distinct concern for the protective parameters of the rule of law, a purposive pursuit of fair outcomes and a commitment to flexible decision making. Examining the characteristics and conditions of this form of justice-oriented administrative action, the book draws together a range of academic studies on public administration across the social sciences and socio-legal studies in a timely and accessible manner and is an essential read for those interested in governance, justice and welfare.

Zach Richards is an author, advocate, public speaker and lecturer. He holds a PhD in Law and Social Theory and Administrative Justice and graduate and undergraduate degrees in Law, Legal Practice and English Literature. He currently lectures in Legal Philosophy, International Human Rights and Administrative Law. Richards is passionate about administrative justice and welfare-oriented governance and is dedicated to supporting causes that advocate for the promotion of human equality.

Responsive Legality
The New Administrative Justice

Zach Richards

Routledge
Taylor & Francis Group
LONDON AND NEW YORK

First published 2019 by Routledge

2 Park Square, Milton Park, Abingdon, Oxfordshire OX14 4RN
52 Vanderbilt Avenue, New York, NY 10017

Routledge is an imprint of the Taylor & Francis Group, an informa business

First issued in paperback 2019

British Library Cataloguing-in-Publication Data
A catalogue record for this book is available from the British Library

Library of Congress Cataloging-in-Publication Data
Names: Richards, Zach, author.
Title: Responsive legality : the new administrative justice / Zach Richards.
Description: New York : Routledge, 2018. | Includes index.
Identifiers: LCCN 2018016874 | ISBN 9781138592742 (hbk)
Subjects: LCSH: Justice, Administration of. | Administrative procedure. | Administrative law.
Classification: LCC K3410 .R53 2018 | DDC 342/.06—dc23
LC record available at https://lccn.loc.gov/2018016874

ISBN: 978-1-138-59274-2 (hbk)
ISBN: 978-0-367-89530-3 (pbk)

Typeset in Galliard
by Apex CoVantage, LLC

Contents

Acknowledgements

My thanks are owed to the many friends and colleagues who have helped give life to this book over the last number of years.

Many thanks to Theunis Roux, Arthur Glass, Martin Krygier, Bronwen Morgan, Cameron Holley, Trish Luker, Jenni Millbank, Jill Hunter, Bettina Lange, Anthony Bradney, Wibren Van Der Berg, Marc Hertogh, Marie-Andree Jacob, Susan Silbey, Trish Luker, Amanda Wilson and Kenneth Winston for your helpful comments, discussions and suggestions.

I am grateful to Jenny Jarrett for your tireless support and the many talented University of New South Wales (UNSW) friends and researchers who began this journey with me over heated debates and spilled wines.

Thank you to Marie-Louise Taylor for your copyediting and my research assistants at Keele University Adam Mawardi and Megan Davidson for your proofreading. Thanks also to Scott Cummins and Sara Dehm for your generous proofreading and comments on initial versions.

I am glad to have worked on aspects of the project as a visiting doctoral candidate at the Centre for Socio-Legal Studies at the University of Oxford and thankful to UNSW for the generous funding to do so.

Thanks to the many participants who commented on and improved this work in the Administrative Justice stream at the Annual Socio-Legal Studies conferences UK 2014, 2015, 2017 and 2018 and the Annual Law and Society of Australia and New Zealand Conference 2014.

Thank you to the institutions I have worked in that helped form my early thinking on the subject, especially the Policy, Innovation, Research and Evaluation Unit of the Department of Immigration and Citizenship, Canberra, and the University of Sydney for their research secondment funding for this placement, as well as the Supreme Court NSW.

Thank you to my parents Deborah and Peter for instilling in me a love of learning and appetite for knowledge and my brothers Will and James for the many happy childhood adventures and memories.

Many thanks to the team at Routledge who have helped make publication a pleasurable and seamless affair and to Jennifer Bonnar for project managing the final manuscript.

And, of course, sincere thanks to the interviewed participants of the Refugee Review Tribunal of Australia – whose observed dedication to their work and cause bring diffuse bodies of literature to life, illuminating rich and hopeful present and future potentialities for twenty-first-century justice.

1 The new administrative justice

Responsive legality for twenty-first-century justice

This book presents a theory of administrative justice for the twenty-first-century: responsive legality. It argues that responsive legality is the characteristically new justifying logic of twenty-first-century administrative action, which reflects significant and largely positive developments from previous twentieth-century features. It is new, and it is better than what we had before. That said, it is not perfect, and its limitations should be lamented to remind us that where quests for justice in public administration are concerned, we might always hope for better.

So, what is responsive legality? When responsive legality is at play, public officials value responsive, adaptive engagement with the needs of the applicant; they strive to balance procedural and substantive justice; they draw on the cognitive techniques of applying experience and verifying the truth; and they demonstrate a dual valuation of the rule of law and orientation towards an ethic of care. Officials work in this mode to apply their intuition, perception and tacit knowledge. They respond flexibly and adaptively to changed circumstances in pursuit of procedurally fair and substantively just outcomes. Responsive legality can exist both within the organisation as a whole, and in the individual psyche of officials working within those organisations. It can exist in private and public organisations; though the emphasis of this book is on its existence in public organisations because of the added welfare benefits it can produce for applicants in those contexts.

As this book explores, the core features of responsive legality include the following:

1 Decision making is motivated by the legitimating value of responsiveness.
2 Decision making is *generally concerned* with concepts of social welfare and well-being, demonstrating the hallmarks of higher-level leadership.
3 Decision making is driven by the master ideal of legality: it aspires to rule conformity to avoid archaic, repressive governance.
4 Decision making is value-driven, particularly adopting a preference for personal experience and truth-verifying abilities as the preferred cognitive decision-making techniques.

This ideal type – typifying these cumulative justificatory logics – is represented visually in Table 1.1.

The discernment of responsive legality stems from the overwhelming evidence in the public administration literature, which when drawn together reveals that exponential changes over the early twenty-first century have brought with them new 'interactive' forms of organisation, forms that (new or not)[1] need to be accounted for in recognising what is distinct and important about twenty-first-century administrative justice.

Included within far-reaching interdisciplinary discussions of contemporary public administration (from socio-legal administrative justice studies to knowledge management in organisation studies to law and society scholarship) are several notions: that there is a high degree of conflict, excitement and unanticipated change evident in contemporary organisations;[2] that individual team consensus is becoming more important than relying on hierarchy or authority;[3] that responsiveness and organic emotionality drive workplace norms;[4] and that there is a high level of personal involvement of career-level civil servants in administrative decision making.[5]

It has been argued that 'modern bureaucracies are under reconstruction'[6] where decision making is becoming increasingly purposive, with an emphasis on considering the reason behind the rules rather than the rules themselves;[7] it is also evident where the decision-making power of individuals is no longer derived from the official rank of the individual but from the nature of the problem at hand.[8] Even more emphatically, it has been put that 'of all areas of political science, no other has undergone a transformation comparable to that experienced by public administration over the past twenty years'[9] and that this has effectively meant that 'all of the essential truths that guided practising public administrators and students of administration have now been challenged and often replaced'.[10] There is a generalised pattern of agreement that the common features of twenty-first-century public administration include a growth in creativity in public organisations, where rule-bound behaviour is being replaced with a core focus on individual initiative, purposive decision making and applicant care.[11]

These discussions in recent public administration literature and a related sub-branch of literature that examines knowledge circulation within public organisations – knowledge management (KM) studies – explored in depth in Chapters 2 and 5, are consistent with a number of socio-legal studies which have noted that

Table 1.1 Responsive legality

Model	*Legitimating Value/Goal*	*Equality Orientation*	*Cognitive Techniques*	*Mode of Decision Making*
Responsive Legality	Responsiveness	Substantive Fairness and Procedural Justice	Truth Verification and Applying Experience	Protecting Welfare through Rule of Law

an organic range of human values is increasingly guiding administrative officials in making their decisions.[12] Public officials have been found to be infused with a 'personalistic value orientation',[13] whereby decision making is increasingly driven by responsiveness and an orientation towards equality.[14] Often, public administrators first make moral judgements about applicants and then mould or abandon particular rules and organisational procedures to support their own moral goals.[15] The modern office has increasingly become an adaptive product that naturally responds to social needs and pressures.[16] 'Leaders' at these higher levels of the organisation are not only concerned with efficiency maximisation; they are additionally concerned with maintaining group well-being.[17] Across all levels of government, there is a kind of work being done to meet social needs that is not equivalent to office holding or high prestige and involves individuals who are primarily experts in promoting and protecting human values.[18]

In presenting responsive legality, Chapter 2 of this book introduces recent administrative developments observed in public administration and socio-legal administrative justice literature, noting some of the distinctions between traditional predominant modes of governance and the separate typifying features of twenty-first-century governance.

Chapter 3 introduces the fieldwork site where the empirical component of the research for this book was conducted: the Refugee Review Tribunal of Australia (RRT). It uses the RRT as a site to illuminate some of the component features of the type – though it must be stressed from the outset that this study is presented to illustrate to readers the features of the type and how it plays out in reality, rather than as rigid generalisable proof of the existence of the type, which must be holistically gathered from the studies explored throughout the book. The chapter provides a descriptive background to the operations of the RRT and its place in the Australian legal system and a brief discussion of the core reasons why this site was suited for illuminating responsive legality.

Chapter 4 explores the core motivating value of responsive legality: responsiveness. It argues that when justifying their decisions according to this type, public officials and the organisations that they work in value responsiveness in that they cling to a generalisation of purpose that aims to distinguish what is truly necessary for each particular applicant rather than what is taken for granted in traditions and routines. In this, they deeply value flexibility and adaptability and aim to deal with situations on a case-by-case basis, drawing firm justification for their decision from the extent to which they were able to holistically respond to the overall set of circumstances in each individual case.

Chapter 5 discusses the dual equality orientation of responsive legality: a joint striving towards procedural fairness and substantive justice. On one hand, public officials and organisations recognise the fundamental importance of rule-of-law compliance and the importance of applying and following organisational and broader jurisdictional rules for the promotion of democratic values and societal cohesion. However, to achieve a real sense of fairness for applicants and surpass the limitations of a rigid and somewhat socially blind rule-of-law compliance they must also strive for substantive justice, which means embracing a concern for equality of outcome and surpassing the limitations of equality of opportunity in its narrow emphasis on consistency of treatment through rigid rule conformity.

Chapter 6 discusses the cognitive techniques applied in responsive legality: a combination of applying experience and verifying the truth. It discusses the ways that public officials and organisations can and are positively embracing the benefits of individuals' tacit, intuitive, experiential knowledge. In a generally positive fashion they are increasingly celebrating the application of diverse knowledge bases (in contradistinction from more traditional twentieth-century emphases on explicit formal and codified knowledge applications) to produce the system goals of substantive and procedural fairness that this new form of administrative justice strives towards.

Chapter 7 explores the mode of responsive legality: protecting applicant welfare through applying the rule of law. It argues that when justifying their decisions according to this type, decision makers are generally concerned with the welfare of the applicant and acknowledge that this welfare will be achieved, in part, at least, through rule-of-law compliance. In this discussion, the chapter draws on the socio-legal legal consciousness framework[19] to consider the nuanced relationships between officials' legal attitudes and justice orientations. It argues that officials who strategically use the law to achieve positive outcomes for applicants – when also demonstrating the other component features of responsive legality – come significantly further in promoting positive visions of administrative justice than in moments when they position themselves 'against the law', or – acting *only* in their own self-interest – 'with the law', thus tainting the administration in these moments with the features of self-serving rule-of-law compliance.

Twentieth-century administration: public governance in context

In providing the social and cultural context for the twenty-first-century emergence of responsive legality, we might first consider the predominant mode of twentieth-century administrative justice: bureaucratic rationality, which provides a clear departure point for the emergence of the responsive-legality type.

The starting foundation of twentieth-century conceptions of administrative justice is Max Weber's *Economy and Society*,[20] which famously refers to an 'iron cage' of far-reaching bureaucratic rationalisation, argued to be the most efficient and formally rational way of organising human behaviour. According to Weber, twentieth-century administration is characterised by six core principles: it involves a fixed and official jurisdictional area generally ordered by rules, laws or administrative regulations; it operates according to principles of office hierarchy and levels of graded authority where there is supervision of lower offices by higher offices; management of the office is based on written documents; it requires office management that presupposes thorough and expert training; when the office is fully developed, official activity requires the full working capacity of the official; and the management of the office follows general rules, which are more or less stable and involve jurisprudence or administrative or business management, and which can be learnt.

For Weber, public administration has a formally articulated and differentiated structure. Formal rules delimit the 'jurisdictional area of each agency, specify the distribution of authority within the agency, spell out the duties associated with each position, and establish a regular procedure for carrying out these duties'.[21] Within this system, formal, abstract and general rules are the specific means of bureaucratic administration. The formalism of administration is expressed in a distinctive detached bureaucratic ethos. It is devoted to 'impersonal and functional purposes',[22] where the official acts in a 'spirit of formalistic impersonality . . . without hatred or passion, and hence without affection or enthusiasm'.[23] This formalistic impersonality corresponds with the pure instrumentalism and impersonality of market transactions and money contracts, and the execution of official business 'without regard for persons'[24] aligns to the formal equality of all persons in the modern legal order. As such, the central component of twentieth-century public administration for Weber was the differentiation of person from office: jobs were defined by the needs of the organisation rather than the people in them.

In this distinctively impersonal and rational ethos, Weber's twentieth-century official acts like a machine. They act with precision, speed, unambiguity, continuity, unity, strict subordination and the reduction of friction and material and personal costs. The predictable mechanical efficiency of rule-bound administration 'makes possible a particularly high degree of calculability of results',[25] which advantages capitalist entrepreneurs who 'must be able to count on . . . the rational, predictable functioning of . . . administrative agencies'.[26]

Calling into question the twentieth-century 'uniqueness' of this phenomena, Guy Peters and Vincent Wright highlight that whilst the principle in the public sector of direct control or hierarchy is often associated with Weber, the principle is actually much older. It was one of the originating principles of the Napoleonic administrative model of France and several other European countries and is premised on the need and willingness of people in public organisations to follow orders given by their superiors within the organisation.[27] However, whether or not there were remnants of bureaucratic rationality that predated the twentieth century in which they flourished, there can be no doubt that this model of public administration indeed dominated and flourished in twentieth-century conditions and discourse. It was unambiguously, the ideal-typical modus operandi of twentieth-century Western governance, though it can be traced to locations and times that far predated it.

Whilst Weber's work on bureaucratic rationality has been widely critiqued for its Eurocentrism and cultural pessimism,[28] it nevertheless remains a pioneering and foundational descriptive account of administration in modernity that has critically survived the critique of its discontents.[29]

Presenting a more normatively driven and cynical perspective of bureaucratic rationality in administration than Weber, Robert Merton's analysis of 'bureaucratic personality'[30] stands as the classic statement of the dysfunctional consequences of bureaucracy. Merton presents an astute early account of some of the limitations of bureaucratic rationality, including that the rigid attachment to formal rules and regulations can give rise to a bureaucratic personality type that becomes obsessed with procedural compliance. Clearly problematically – for the organisation and the user of the justice system – the bureaucratic personality type insists on the unconditional conformity to rules and procedures, regardless of whether they actually enhance the goals of the organisation. When rules become a means in and of themselves, they take on a ritualistic, rather than a rational, character. This ironically and problematically encourages both the displacement of goals and a socially blind adherence to methods and procedures at the expense of the larger organisational purpose.

A shifting landscape: late twentieth-century developments

Noting something different to what had been described by Weber in earlier accounts of mechanical twentieth-century modernist bureaucracy, Philip Selznick presented some of the first accounts of the role of non-robotic human values in public administration. For Selznick, the logic of efficiency 'loses its force'[31] as we approach the top of the organisation; Weberian metaphors of mechanical rationality in bureaucracy become less significant the higher up the bureaucratic ranks one progresses. Selznick argued that late twentieth-century organisations were more diverse than Weber's bureaucratic rationality model suggested. What's more, he noted that there was an important normative component missing from Weber's account; where Weber sought to observe and describe the core features of public administration for the twentieth century, Selznick was also interested in presenting a value judgement on these issues, discerning not just what *was* the case but also whether, and *why*, these governance structures were conducive to the production of a range of administrative justice outcomes.

In so evaluating, Selznick argued that organisations as rational tools that are judged by their efficiency alone are merely 'expendable tools'.[32] On the other hand, he found much to celebrate in organisations composed of cognisant individuals with differing ideals and motives. Here, decision makers and organisations are 'infused with value'.[33] This form of organisation, in fact, becomes a higher form of social entity: it becomes an institution. The late twentieth-century organisation was marked as an adaptive and responsive product that naturally responds to social needs and pressures. 'Leaders' at these higher levels are not merely concerned with mechanically performing routine tasks in the interests of efficiency maximisation; they are additionally concerned with maintaining group well-being. In this concept of higher-level leadership, leadership specifically involves a kind of work done to meet social needs that is not equivalent to office holding or high prestige or decision making but involves individuals who are primarily 'experts in the promotion and protection of values'.[34]

Taking these claims further, Alvin Gouldner and Peter Blau, two of Merton's students alongside Selznick, considered the role that bureaucratic personality played in contributing to organisational dysfunction.[35] They found that apart from bureaucratic personality alone – many organisational dysfunctions also derived from distinctly human qualities: they derived, in part, from human resistance, conflict, innovation and opposition as much as over conformity to prescriptive norms.

Apart from exploring contemporary changes in bureaucratic goals, cognitions and behaviour, organisational scholars have also proposed various models of macro-level structural change, embodying radically new administrative types. One well-known conceptualisation[36] is found in Henry Mintzberg's work on adhocracy, which refers to agencies that have simply organically grown, without much explicit design.[37] These settings are characterised by a lack of structure and formal rules and are epitomised in small creative agencies such as the design studio and have proliferated in the last two decades. Another modern organisational variation is presented by William Ouchi, who discusses the emergences of the "clan" based on a shared culture rather than formal rules, metaphorically encompassed in the way members of an extended anthropological clan might function in traditional society.[38] In variation again, Gunnar Hedlund coins the term 'heterarchy', which is a form of organisation that involves plural connections between individual members rather than a single chain of authority in more traditional types of organisation. Epitomising this structure are professional firms such as law partnerships, where individuals engage within and across the partner companies.[39] There are also entirely new organisational and governance structures such as the postmodern organisation, which is, in essence, a bureaucratic organisation that has undergone a degree of de-differentiation of its structure; it has become more integrated, more team-based and less specialist.[40] Closely linked are new and emerging online communities and organisations, which are sometimes entirely linked and driven through virtual networks rather than formal rules; these also often involve several seemingly separate organisations that are actually linked through online relationships, seen for example in architect or other design studios working on large projects with specialist partners.[41]

Selznick's later work with Phillipe Nonet[42] also explores contemporary variations of bureaucratic modes of governance and was 'quasi evolutionary'[43] in explicitly discussing and defining the notion of post-bureaucratic organisation succeeding bureaucratic and pre-bureaucratic forms. Within this conceptualisation, the post-bureaucratic type is mission oriented and flexible rather than jurisdictional and fixed; its authority structure is based on project teams and task forces, open communication, the diffusion of authority, and substantive rationality, rather than on a hierarchy involving formal-legal rationality. In managing its operations, its rules are subordinated to the purpose, with an avoidance of rule rigidity; its decision-making style is participatory and problem-centred, with broad delegation, and its careers are characterised by multiple and temporary affiliations with reliance on sub-contracting and experts who have an autonomous professional base.

For Selznick, the totality of the contemporary organisation's rational and normative characteristics form a "distinctive competence"[44] that makes it unique. The core components of this competence are a clearly defined mission and an embodiment of the missions' values within the overall fabric of the institution,[45] which results in members being personally and productively enveloped in these values as they execute policy for the benefit of the organisation and the individuals it serves.[46]

Twentieth-century models of administrative justice

Exploring the traditional socio-legal models of administrative justice

These broader contemporary organisational changes have given rise to discussions across a range of social scientific fields regarding new forms of administrative justice operating within these organisations. One illuminating framework that responsive legality draws from is the discussion of models of administrative justice in socio-legal studies. The following discussion provides an outline of the three key models of administrative justice presented in this discussion and how responsive legality relates to each of these models.

Jerry Mashaw's bureaucratic justice

Mashaw's study into Social Security disability claims in the US Disability Discrimination Administration (DDA), *Bureaucratic Justice*,[47] provides an influential twentieth-century socio-legal model of administrative justice. Perhaps unsurprisingly in the context of the broader social scientific discussion of twentieth- and late twentieth-century structural governance changes, Mashaw found that 'organisations and the bureaucrats who inhabit them have their own goals, desires and motivations'.[48] His study reveals that the social security administration in the US had generated its own highly individualised internal law of administration that could only be understood through penetrating the administration itself, yet the findings of the study are said to have wider theoretical application across a range of administrative decision-making contexts.

Mashaw constructs three models of administrative justice, each with their own goals, and approaches to framing the administrative questions to be decided, different techniques for resolving those questions and various decision-making approaches that describe those features of the model. According to Mashaw, bureaucracies operate according to one of three models, in the sense that they generally conform to most of these characteristics most of the time. Whilst the features represent central tendencies, they might also shade into each other at the margins.

(A) BUREAUCRATIC RATIONALITY

When driven by bureaucratic rationality, decisions are justified according to the overarching values of accuracy and efficiency. In other words, a decision will be thought to be justified if it predominantly strives to be factually correct and to have been made with minimal burdens on time and minimal resource constraints for the organisation. In discerning if something is 'factually correct', the decision maker must distinguish between true or false claims. To facilitate this process, the decision-making environment must be focused on factual and technocratic decision making. In conforming to these legitimating values, the primary goal is to follow a designated programme implemented by the organisation, rather than striving for client satisfaction (as in the professional treatment model) or conflict resolution (as in the moral judgement model). In doing so, this model regards questions of values or subjective preferences as irrelevant to the core decision-making task in the belief that the legislature should already have decided value questions. Any designation of this determination of value into the administrative decision-making process would effectively involve the reallocation of decision-making authority from the bureau to individuals, which would prevent the over-arching determination of whether adjudicative action does, in fact, accord with a true state in the world.

In place of value-driven decision making, bureaucratic rationality thrives within a hierarchical programme structure and involves decision making through the application of information processing as its core cognitive technique. This is captured in Weber's summary that 'bureaucratic administration means fundamentally domination through knowledge',[49] meaning that knowledge in the bureaucratic ideal type is structured according to the specialisation and division of labour coordinated via rules and hierarchical lines of authority.

To illustrate, Mashaw suggests a motor safety inspection bureau as a site in which bureaucratic rationality readily operates. According to this model, the decision-making goal of ensuring that unsafe vehicles are kept off the road might rely on an essentially objective definition of 'safe' in terms of certain mechanical or physical characteristics, and it is the task of the decision maker to rationally and routinely assess these characteristics rather than superimpose their own subjective judgement.

(B) PROFESSIONAL TREATMENT

The second administrative justice model that Mashaw constructs is professional treatment. Professional treatment is exemplified in public hospitals and legal service agencies where the service ideal drives decision making and where the professional defines and legitimises the agency. The core feature of this model is that good professional judgement is considered to be an adequate explanation for a decision being made. The model is exemplified in medicine, but it is also a defining characteristic of law and the Christian ministry and new and emerging professions such as social work.

For a decision to be truly justified under professional treatment, the decision maker must serve the client and strive towards the elimination of the complaints presented to her by her clients. In this process, she must tailor advice to her own resources: the constraints on professional service are conceptualised as trade-offs between competitive options with and between various clients, rather than trade-offs between professional services and other social values.

In contrast to bureaucratic rationality, professional treatment recognises the incompleteness of facts, the intuitive nature of judgement, and the singularity of individual contexts. In Mashaw's fieldwork context, disability decisions justified according to professional treatment are viewed as prognoses of the probable effects of disease or trauma on functioning, rather than attempts to establish the credibility of facts. This involves an emphasis on therapeutic and vocational prospects and a prioritisation of personal examination and counselling where 'the professional combines his or her own observations and experience to reach conclusions that are as much art as science'.[50]

The core technique underpinning professional treatment is therefore to apply appropriate professional knowledge to each particular problem. The administrative structure when operating under this model would direct claimant clients to multi-professional centres so that they can be assisted through examination and counselling. Rules of substance and procedure, hierarchy and efficiency are all subordinated to the norms of the professional culture, creating a lateral network rather than a hierarchical command centre for the organisation. In this, there is some similarity between the bureaucratic rationality and the professional treatment models: both expect that the decision maker is in command of a specialised body of knowledge and that they apply their expert judgement to the problem at hand. However, a core difference between the two models remains: where the rational bureaucrat displays her knowledge through technocratic procedures that are designed to connect concrete decisions with legislatively mandated policy, the scientific art of the professional remains elusive to the layperson. Yet, this elusiveness is justified under professional treatment because the professional decision maker (exemplified by the priest, physician or lawyer) exudes a mystery that is legitimised by the trust implicit in the professional–client relationship. It is in situations where this unique relationship is forged and the trustee acts in the service-oriented interests of the beneficiary client that the greatest justice, under this model, is seen to be done.

(C) MORAL JUDGEMENT

Mashaw's third model of administrative justice, moral judgement, involves correctly allocating benefits and burdens in order to resolve rights disputes. Whilst both bureaucratic rationality and moral judgement involve a belief in the importance of 'getting the facts right', moral judgement differs in that it views decision making as value defining. It strives to give applicants what is perceived to be what they deserve. In this endeavour, the decision maker must remain neutral in that they cannot be connected with the relevant parties or events surrounding the claim in any way that would impair their ability to make an independent decision on the facts presented to them. In this, there is no generalised conception of applicant deservingness; rather, the decision maker must resolve particular claims in a way that fairly allocates benefits and burdens to those individuals.

Mashaw explains that in this model decision makers each apply a general statute and elaborate, via contested cases, the operational content of concepts such as fairness or the public interest. The justice in this model derives from the promise of full and equal opportunity for applicants to receive their entitlements.

(D) INTERPLAY OF MASHAW'S MODELS

One of Mashaw's insights is that the various models of administrative justice are competitive rather than mutually exclusive. According to Mashaw, bureaucracies operate according to one of the three models, in the sense that they generally conform to most of the model's characteristics most of the time. Whilst the features represent central tendencies, they might also shade into each other at the margins. For example, Mashaw found that bureaucratic rationality was the dominant modality in the DDA, and professional treatment and moral judgement played supporting roles. He concluded that when the study was carried out in the early 1980s, bureaucratic rationality was the dominant model and that, notwithstanding variations between and within different countries, it has always been the dominant model when it comes to social security administration.

Mashaw's approach overall is a pluralistic one in the sense that it recognises a plurality of normative positions and acknowledges that situations that are attractive to some people may be unattractive for others. The trade-offs that are made in negotiating decisions according to the different models reflect the concerns and bargaining strength of individuals who have an interest in promoting each of the models.

Michael Adler's models of administrative justice

Adler begins by recognising the attractive features of Mashaw's work. He argues that the overriding benefit of Mashaw's approach is that it recognises that different models of administrative justice co-exist and that each of them is associated with a different way of thinking about administrative justice.

However, Adler also identifies a number of limitations in Mashaw's models and addresses these limitations by modifying and extending them in a number of respects. First, he re-characterises the 'models' as ideal types. This is an important improvement in terminology, as it manages to capture Mashaw's finding that the various models can exist simultaneously and blur into one another at the margins and is helpfully replicated in the later work of Kagan.[51] It is also the approach adopted in exploring the more far-reaching and characteristically twenty-first-century tendency towards responsive legality in this book.

Furthermore, Adler renames Mashaw's models: bureaucratic rationality becomes bureaucratic, professional treatment becomes professional and moral judgement becomes legal.[52] He also re-characterises the models according to their characteristic mode of decision making, their legitimating values, their mode of accountability and their mode of redress. He then adds three additional categories: managerial, consumerist and market.

Adler initially developed and tested an early version of these models through four pieces of research undertaken over fifteen years, from 1988 to 2003. This research included studying the impact of computerisation on social security in the UK, decision making in the Scottish prison system, the assessment of special educational needs in England and Scotland and the computerisation of social security in thirteen countries. Each study aimed to specify various models of administrative justice and collect data to assess the varying strengths of these types. The fieldwork in the four education authorities produced rich accounts of the ways in which trade-offs between normative types of decision making structured the relationships between stakeholders (parents, professionals and officials) in different ways. In each case, an attempt was made to specify a number of different ideal types of administrative justice and to analyse the strength of these types through data collection.

The empirical research found that the bureaucratic, legal and consumerist types had more descriptive purchase in England than in Scotland. This led to the conclusion that the position in England was more complex than in Scotland because more types were currently in play. It was suggested that Scotland might learn more from England by strengthening those types that would shift the balance of power towards parents and children who were in a weak position (presumably legal and consumerist for their emphasis on asserting rights and consumer participation). Thus, for example, a more robust system of appeals might be introduced, and public access to information might be improved. This research was therefore able to provide localised policy-related suggestions for change whilst also having more general theoretical application outside the contexts studied.

There is much that is important and attractive about Adler's revised types. For one, the re-characterisation of Mashaw's 'moral judgement' into 'legal' makes necessary progress, especially in terms of its re-characterisation of legitimating goals. As Adler points out, Mashaw's characterisation of fairness as the legitimising goal of moral judgement begs the question: What is the difference between asking, 'What is just?' – the overall question that each of the models seeks to answer – and 'What is fair?' – the allegedly more distinct question motivating the legitimating goal of moral judgement only? He argues that the association of fairness with the moral judgement model is unfortunate; it narrowly suggests that the other two models are 'unfair' when this is, in fact, what each conception of administrative justice seeks to achieve (drawing on different conceptions of 'fairness').

Second, Adler's approach improves on Mashaw's in that it extends its exclusively internal orientation, making new reference to external mechanisms for redressing problems. This change is important because, as Adler outlines, internal and external procedures should not be seen as alternatives, and for good reasons, they are frequently combined. Adler argues that Mashaw is too cynical about the role of external accountability systems in the production of administrative justice and that whilst it may be the case that officials 'continually face decisions for which external standards provide no binding, perhaps no relevant guidelines', it does not follow that external standards play no role at all in setting standards for decision makers.

Furthermore, Adler's addition of the managerial, consumerist and market types reflects some important changes that have taken place since Mashaw wrote *Bureaucratic Justice*. As Adler explores, the managerial model can be characterised in terms of managerial autonomy, efficiency gains as the legitimating goal, the use of performance indicators to assess accountability and publicity as the characteristic remedy. Consumerism has been a central reference point in the drive for a range of UK public-sector reforms from the mid-1980s onwards. It embodies a view that the service user is an engaged participant in the process rather than a passive recipient of bureaucratic, professional or managerial decisions. It is accordingly characterised in terms of the ongoing participation of consumers in decision making, consumer satisfaction, the introduction of consumer 'charters', the use of consumer 'voice' and the possibility of obtaining compensation for breach of standards in the consumer charters.

In the market model, the administrative system is driven by the goal of competitiveness, and the citizen is perceived as a rational customer who chooses between a range of service providers. The goal for decisions justified on this basis is therefore to make services attractive to as wide a range of service users as possible.

Adler's types also improve on Mashaw's models in that they are able to assess the absolute strength of each conception of administrative justice. Adler posits that in assessing the relative influence of the various models, Mashaw ignores the absolute strength of each. He illustrates the problems associated with this approach, discussing that were the three models given weights of 30, 20 and 10 units and 3, 2 and 1 units, respectively, although the relative strengths of the three models would be the same, their absolute strengths would clearly be very different. Furthermore, Adler's types explicitly recognise the important ways that trade-offs between different types are made in terms of the bargaining strength of those individuals who have particular interests in promoting them: civil servants and bureaucrats in the case of the bureaucratic type, professionals and street-level bureaucrats in the case of the professional type, lawyers and court and tribunal personnel in the case of the legal type, management consultants in the case of the managerial type, consumers and members of the public in the case of the consumerist type and private-sector owners, managers and shareholders in the case of the market type.

Adler appreciates that his models have been subject to some criticism, recognising the critique of Simon Halliday, for example, who has argued that they are not as 'distinct and robust as those of Mashaw'[53] and that they merely constitute a single mode of administrative decision making that is now widely known as the 'New Public Management'.

Adler responds to Halliday with the contention that, whilst the New Public Management is a composite model, best thought of as a 'trade-off' between managerialist, consumerist and market models, each of its components can still exist on its own and is analytically distinct in a number of respects. He argues that whilst each of the components is frequently combined in reality to provide a good account of the 'New Public Management', they need not always present together. Rather, they are 'competitive' in Mashaw's sense in that they each have their own internal logic.

Robert Kagan's regulatory justice

Kagan presents yet another view of administrative justice,[54] which offers a framework for understanding how Mashaw's models of justice relate to one another.

Kagan constructs two new dimensions: participatory/hierarchy and legal formality/legal informality. With respect to participatory/hierarchy, hierarchically organised administrative systems are organised by officials who are relatively immune to pressures stemming from individual applicants or regulated entities and are structured according to case-by-case decision-making procedures. On the other hand, participatory decision-making processes involve individuals or organisations that are subject to the agency's decisions and have their own opportunities to make arguments to each other and to other officials – effectively influencing agency decisions.

In relation to legal formality versus informality, administrative policy implementation varies in terms of the extent to which substantive decisions and procedures are structured via, and expected to conform to, written legal rules. Where the legal rules are more detailed, they are also more 'formal' or 'legalistic'. On the other hand, administrative decision makers are granted more discretion in 'informal' processes, and guiding legal rules are more substantively and procedurally general.

Kagan outlines that an administrative process involving a high degree of hierarchical authority and legal formality involves the uniform implementation of centrally devised rules, vertical accountability and official responsibility for fact-finding. The more hierarchical the system, the less of a role there is for legal representation and influence by conflicting interests of affected citizens.

On the other hand, adversarial legalism refers to decision processes that are constrained by formal procedural rules but where there is weak hierarchy. Kagan outlines that adversarial legalism might help describe the events discussed in Nonet's *Administrative Justice*,[55] for example, where Nonet explores the manner in which California's workers compensation administration was originally designed to provide insurance benefits to injured workers without generating costly legal conflict but was then transformed over time into a highly adversarial and legalistic system as a consequence of ongoing judicial appeals and persistent advocacy by claimants' lawyers. He explains that many agencies, such as the California workers administration, entrust decisions to experts or rule-bound bureaucrats but allow appeals to semi-independent 'administrative law judges' who follow adversarial procedures with active participation by conflicting lawyers.

Kagan's third administrative justice type is negotiation or mediation, which allows organisations and individuals within those organisations who either rely on or resist the agency's authority to present and argue their case informally. For example, when operating within this mode, officials who are required to implement consumer protection law or anti-discrimination law tend to mediate disputes between a claimant and an employer to create a negotiation for settlement.

Fourth, expert or political judgement involves decision processes that are hierarchical, whereby the authority for the decision derives from the professional or political judgement of individual officials and involves nonconformity with detailed legal rules.

Kagan claims that many administrative decisions do not precisely resemble any of the ideal types of expert or political judgement/negotiation or mediation/bureaucratic legalism or adversarial legalism but, rather, combine some elements of two or more types. As Halliday and Scott argue, whilst at first glance separate, the comparative study of Mashaw's and Kagan's models, in fact, reveals a number of similarities: when we superimpose Kagan's dimensions onto Mashaw's schema, we can observe that Mashaw's bureaucratic rationality corresponds with Kagan's category of bureaucratic legalism, both adopting a combination of hierarchy and legal formality; professional treatment corresponds to Kagan's category of expert or political judgement, both adopting a combination of hierarchy and legal informality; and moral judgement corresponds to adversarial legalism, both adopting a combination of participation and legal formality.

Twenty-first-century administrative justice innovations

When the contemporary public administration studies, introduced briefly in this chapter and explored more fully throughout the remainder of the book are examined, we can see that an overall shift occurs from twentieth- to twenty-first-century public administration that involves a movement from bureaucratic rationality as the archetypal mode in twentieth-century governance to responsive legality in the twenty-first. Whilst there is some micro-level detail from the previous models that is unavoidably lost in noting and exploring this shift, the benefits from this broader macro-level analysis derive from the socio-theoretical generalisability that is gained from scrutinising this overall movement.

This broad shift cultural shift from bureaucratic rationality to responsive legality is represented in Table 1.2.

Just as Mashaw imported Weber's twentieth-century conception of bureaucratic rationality[56] into his pioneering bureaucratic rationality model in *Bureaucratic Justice*,[57] this book imports features of Nonet and Selznick's visionary

Table 1.2 Comparing twentieth- and twenty-first-century administrative justice

Model	*Mode*	*Legitimating Value/Goal*	*Equality Orientation*	*Cognitive Techniques*
Bureaucratic Rationality	Applying Rules	Accuracy and Efficiency	Procedural Compliance	Information Processing
Responsive Legality	Protecting Welfare through Rule of Law	Responsiveness	Procedural Compliance and Substantive Fairness	Truth Verification and Applying Experience

conception of responsive law and the broader public administration and case-study evidence[58] to discern responsive legality as the iconic twenty-first-century ideal type of administrative justice.

As can be seen from the table presented, the immediate ways in which responsive legality is distinct from the other normative bases on which administrative decisions are justified are fairly self-evident. However, it could perhaps be argued that these features, on the deeper conceptual level (and not just in terms of the words that are used), only really capture a mishmash of elements of what has already been found. At first fleeting glance, it could, for example, be put that 'protecting welfare through the rule of law' is essentially a blend of Mashaw's bureaucratic rationality (applying rules) and moral judgement (resolving conflict) and Adler's legal (asserting rights).

Certainly, responsive legality is most closely correlated with Adler's legal type in this sense – they share an emphasis on asserting rights/protecting welfare through the application of law. Perhaps this similarity is a reflection of the relatively small time gap between which Adler's type (1988–2003) and this type (2013–2016) were derived. However, there is something essentially different between asserting rights and protecting welfare. The content of rights, whilst itself an incredibly fraught and, of course, much-discussed topic – at least for our purposes here in understanding it in combination with the legal type – suggests an inherent connection with prescriptive legal entitlements as opposed to responsive legality's emphasis on welfare, which labours towards broader notions of therapeutic well-being outside of prescriptive entitlements.[59] This will become clearer in Chapters 4, 5 and 6. However, even if we were to think that asserting rights and protecting welfare were the same thing, it is really the combination of all of these diffuse features of the type – at the same time – that make it cumulatively distinct from the other types and provide the evidence for the descriptive realisation of its impact and importance in twenty-first-century justice.

Furthermore, this book resists the urge to comment on each aspect of the pre-existing and somewhat field specific socio-legal models. This is in part due to the isolated reach of those models, which rely predominantly on the guiding principles of socio-legal studies rather than importing broader public administration and law and social theory frameworks into their development to give them greater cross-disciplinary breadth. It is also because it is hoped that there is a stronger project in discerning something real and new rather than attempting – through artful manipulation of logic and language – to tear down what has gone before. Comparisons are certainly made between aspects of the previous models and the current ideal type of responsive legality, but the goal in making these comparisons is to illuminate the features of the new type and its positive centrality in contemporary governance.

That being said, the model of responsive legality aligns comfortably with the previous models – and, speaking closely to this literature, we can be confident that it has discerned something new. In this, it can bring our understandings of the normative bases on which administrative decision makers justify their decisions markedly further, importantly accommodating aspects of public administration that were not accounted for in these pioneering models.

Responsive legality as an ideal type

Rather than reflecting a basic structural relationship between independent decision makers and expressed ideals – where individual personas are analysed for their different levels of legal identification and correlation with broader values – the central model functions on the level of abstraction, as an ideal-typical model that connects the decision makers' concepts of law with their normative values.

In this sense, the model presented in this book draws on Weber's well-known ideal-typical framework[60] where the analytical construction of the ideal type is formed from characteristics and elements of the phenomena studied but is not meant to correspond to all of the characteristics of any one particular case. The conceptual pattern underpinning the ideal-typical model brings together certain relationships and events of historical complexity to construct a conception of an internally coherent system. The model is under no illusion that the world actually is this neat in reality; rather, it aims to construct order out of chaos by making the characteristic features of the relationships pragmatically clear and understandable. In its conceptual purity, the ideal-typical model cannot be found perfectly in reality, but it can be indispensable for heuristic and expository purposes. As Weber outlines,

> [i]t is constructed through the one-sided accentuation of one or more points of view and the symbol of a great many diffuse, discreet, more or less present and occasionally absent concrete individual phenomena, which are arranged according to those one-sidedly emphasised viewpoints into a unified analytical construct.[61]

Importantly, the ideal-typical model is to be distinguished from a model of what 'ought' to exist: it is an analytical construct that is considered 'ideal' strictly in the logical sense of the term. Of course, this is not to say that this study of decision-maker ideals construes the ideals studied themselves as logical but simply that the heuristic framing of the study is itself analytically derived.

Martin Krygier presents an arresting account of the ideal-typical model, with a normative valuation of its unyielding utility perhaps apparent in his approving poeticism:

> Of course, Weber stressed, such 'ideal types' were nowhere found in unalloyed form. There will always be legacies of earlier forms, impurities, pathologies, corruptions, breakdowns, mixtures. But ideal types are not fantasies. They are disciplined 'as if' thought experiments, intended to lay bare institutional logics immanent in real structures, forms and practices, even if variably mixed and dominant there. Real-world organisations or economies or politics never operate exclusively according to any one such logic. There are typically competing logics at work, some inherited, some on the way in, some on the way out; and there are also other forms of context and circumstance that intervene.[62]

In each of these senses, responsive legality is to be understood in the ideal-typical sense: it is not perfect, pure or logically infallible, but neither is it a futile product of the imagination. It is, as Weber argued, a way of condensing the messiness of one aspect of social reality into a comprehensive analytical form. It is a way of unearthing the common tendencies of the latent social realities studied before the later normative critique can be formed.

Adopting this approach, the empirical component of this book in portions of Chapters 4, 5, 6 and 7 is presented *to illustrate features of the ideal type explored.* Like any ideal type, responsive legality is drawn from a combination of intuitions, conceptual logics and the existing studies. Having been analytically derived, it is explored through the interview data with a view to concretising the discussion and illuminating the component features of the type.

Normative value of responsive legality: celebrating good governance

Having presented the scaffolding to the ideal-typical framework considered in this book, we might now briefly consider the normative position that the book takes in relation to these component features.

The argument put is that contemporary decision makers and agencies increasingly demonstrate the features of responsive legality in preference for twentieth-century bureaucratic rationality, and it is in these moments that they bring the most benefits to the agency and do the most justice for the individuals accessing it. In responsively negotiating the legal and social pressures of the institution and jurisdiction that binds them, they demonstrate a positively flexible disposition that ensures equality of outcome for individuals in preference for a more superficial over-reliance on the production of consistency of results. This allows for a dual attainment of substantive and procedural justice for applicants and the protection and promotion of individual welfare whilst having simultaneous regard for the principles of democratic rule-of-law compliance.

In this, responsive legality comes further than previous modes of governance and administrative justice models in meeting visions of a humane welfare-oriented system of public administration. It is to be observed and celebrated. We might, therefore remember that whilst responsive legality is certainly not present everywhere – its component features provide hope, in their depth, complexity and breadth of application, for twenty-first-century justice.

Notes

1 See Chapter 2 of this book where this point is discussed at length.
2 See, for example, Charles Hecksher, 'Defining the Post Bureaucratic Type' in Charles Heckscher and Anne Donnellon (eds), *The Post Bureaucratic Organisation* (Sage Publications, 1994) 15; see chapter two of this book, 69–71, for further discussion. See also Harro Hopfl, 'Bureaucratic Accountability in Britain: Some Sceptical Reflections' in Stewart Clegg, Martin Harris and Harro Hopfl (eds), *Managing Modernity: Beyond Bureaucracy* (Oxford University Press, 2011).

3 See, for example, Heckscher, above n 2, 24; Hopfl, above n 2, 41; Sharon Bolton, *Emotion Management in the Workplace* (Palgrave Macmillan, 2004) 19; Bill Jenkins and Edward Page (eds), *The Foundations of Bureaucracy in Economic and Social Thought II* (Edward Elgar Publishing, 2005) 565.
4 See, for example, Bolton, above n 3, 13–14; Heckscher, above n 2. These shifts are also consistent with the earlier analytical observations and visionary predictions of Alvin Gouldner, *Patterns of Industrial Democracy* (Free Press, 1954) and Peter Blau, *Bureaucracy in Modern Society* (Random House, 1968).
5 See, for example, Paul Du Gay, 'Without Regard to Persons: Problems of Involvement and Attachment' in Stewart Clegg, Martin Harris and Harro Hopfl (eds), *Managing Modernity: Beyond Bureaucracy* (Oxford University Press, 2011).
6 Stewart Clegg, 'Under Recoruction: Modern Bureaucracies' in Stewart Clegg, Martin Harris and Harro Hopfl (eds), *Managing Modernity: Beyond Bureaucracy* (Oxford University Press, 2011) 202–29.
7 See, for example, Heckscher, above n 2; Chris Jewell, *Agents of the Welfare State: How Caseworkers Respond to Need in the United States, Germany and Sweden* (Palgrave Macmillan, 2007); Du Gay, above n 5; Clegg, above n 6.
8 See, for example, Clegg, above n 5, 205–29.
9 B Guy Peters and Vincent Wright, 'Public Policy and Administration, Old and New' in Robert E Goodin and Hans-Dieter Klingemann (eds), *A New Handbook of Political Science in the Foundations of Bureaucracy in Economic and Social Thought* (Oxford University Press, 1996).
10 Ibid 628.
11 See this book, pages 11 and 29–30, for a discussion of this literature.
12 See, for example, Marc Hertogh, 'Through the Eyes of Bureaucrats: How Frontline Officials Understand Administrative Justice' in Adler (ed), *Administrative Justice in Context* (Hart Publishing, 2010) 203–25; Jewell, above n 7; Steven Maynard-Moody and Michael Musheno, *Cops, Teachers, Councillors: Stories from the Front Line of Public Service* (University of Michigan Press, 2003).
13 Hertogh, above n 12.
14 Ibid.
15 Maynard-Moody and Musheno, above n 12.
16 See Clegg, above n 6; Jewell, above n 7; Peters and Wright, above n 9.
17 See, for example, Heckscher, above n 2, 24; Hopfl, above n 5, 41; Bolton, above n 3, 19; Jenkins and Page, above n 3, 565. For the earliest prominent account of this, see Philip Selznick, *Leadership in Administration* (University of California Press, 1957). See also Philippe Nonet and Philip Selznick, *Law and Society in Transition: Toward Responsive Law* (Harper, 1978), especially 118.
18 See, for example, Hertogh, above n 12; Maynard-Moody and Musheno, above n 12. See also Nonet and Selznick, above n 17, 28; Gouldner, above n 4; Blau, above n 4 for the earliest prominent accounts of this.
19 See this book, pages 19 and 108–131, for an extended discussion of this framework and its applicability to responsive legality.
20 Ibid 54.
21 Max Weber, *Economy and Society* (Harvard University Press, 1978) 235.
22 Ibid 959.
23 Ibid 225.
24 Ibid 600.
25 Ibid 223.
26 Ibid 1095.
27 Peters and Wright, above n 9, 632.
28 See, for example, Harold Berman, 'Some False Premises of Max Weber's Sociology of Law' (1987) 65 *Washington University Law Quarterly* 758; Ferdinand Kolegar,

'The concept of "rationalization" and Cultural Pessimism in Max Weber's Sociology' (2005) 5(4) *Sociological Quarterly* 355; Donald Levine, 'Rationality and Freedom: Weber and Beyond' (1981) 51(1) *Sociological Inquiry* 5; Joyce Sterling and Wilbert Moore, 'Weber's Analysis of Legal Rationalisation: A Critique and Constructive Modification' (1987) 2(1) *Sociological Forum* 667.

29 See, for example, Reinhard Bendix, *Max Weber: An Intellectual Portrait* (University California Press, 1977); Jane Bennett, *The Enchantment of Modern Life: Attachments, Crossings, and Ethics* (Princeton University Press, 2001); Cary Boucock, *In the Grip of Freedom: Law and Modernity in Max Weber* (University of Toronto Press, 2000); Sally Ewing, 'Formal Justice and the Spirit of Capitalism: Max Weber's Sociology of Law' (1987) 21(3) *Law and Society Review* 488; Stephan Feldman, 'An Interpretation of Max Weber's Theory of Law: Metaphysics, Economics and the Iron Cage of Constitutional Law' (1991) *Law and Social Inquiry*, 205; William Hennis, 'Max Weber's "Central Question"' (1983) 12(2) *Economy and Society* 135; Stephen Kalberg, 'Max Weber's Types of Rationality: Cornerstones for the Analysis of Rationalization Processes in History' (1980) 85(5) *American Journal of Sociology* 1145; Antony Kronman, *Max Weber* (Edward Arnold, 1983); Scott Lash and Sam Whimster, *Max Weber, Rationality and Modernity* (Allen & Unwin, 1987); Karl Löwith, *Max Weber and Karl Marx* (Allen & Unwin, 1982); Dragan Milovanovic, *Weberian and Marxist Analysis of Law* (Avebury, 1989); Wolfgang Schluchter, *The Rise of Western Rationalism: Max Weber's Developmental History* (University of California Press, 1981); David Trubek, 'Max Weber on Law and the Rise of Capitalism' (1972) *Wisconsin Law Review* 720.

30 Robert Merton, *Bureaucratic Structure and Personality* (Free Press, 1957).

31 Selznick, above n 18, 3.

32 Ibid 20.

33 Ibid 19.

34 Ibid 28.

35 See Gouldner, above n 4, and Blau, above n 4.

36 For discussion see David Buchanan and Louise Fitzgerald, 'New Lock, New Stock, New Barrel, Same Gun: Accessorised Bureaucracy of Health Care' in Stewart Clegg, Martin Harris and Harro Hopfl (eds), *Managing Modernity: Beyond Bureaucracy* (Oxford University Press, 2011) at 58 and Stewart Clegg, *Under Reconstruction: Modern Bureaucracies* (2011) in Stewart Clegg, Martin Harris and Harro Hopfl (eds), *Managing Modernity: Beyond Bureaucracy* (Oxford University Press 2015).

37 Henry Mintzberg, *Power in and Around Organisations* (Prentice-Hall, 1983).

38 William Ouchi, 'Markets, Bureaucracies and Clans' (1980) 25 *Administrative Science Quarterly* 129.

39 Gunnar Hedland, 'The Hypermodern MNC: A Heterarchy?' (1986) 25(1) *Human Resource Management Journal* 9.

40 Stewart Clegg, *Modern Organisations: Organisation Studies in the Postmodern World* (Sage Publications, 1990).

41 William Davidow and Michael Malone, *The Virtual Corporation: Structuring and Revitalizing the Corporation for the 21st Century* (Harper, 1992).

42 Nonet and Selznick, above n 17.

43 Jenkins and Page, above n 3, 565.

44 Selznick, above n 18 at 139.

45 Ibid 66–7.

46 Ibid 36.

47 Jerry Mashaw, *Bureaucratic Justice* (Yale University Press, 1983) 68.

48 Ibid 213.

49 Weber, above n 21.
50 Ibid 28.
51 Robert Kagan, 'The Organisation of Administrative Justice Systems: The Role of Political Mistrust' in Adler, above n 12.
52 Adler, above n 12, 149.
53 Simon Halliday and Colin Scott, 'A Cultural Analysis of Administrative Justice' in Adler, above n 12 (2010) 183.
54 Kagan, above n 51, 164.
55 Phillippe Nonet, *Administrative Justice* (Russell Sage Foundation, 1969).
56 Weber, above n 21.
57 Mashaw, above n 47.
58 Nonet and Selznick, above n 17.
59 See Chapters 4 and 5 of this book for a detailed discussion of how this is the case.
60 Max Weber, *The Methodology of the Social Sciences* (E A Shils and H A Finch trans and ed, Free Press, 2011) 578 [originally published 1949] 90–112.
61 Ibid.
62 Martin Krygier, *Ideals in the World* (Stanford University Press, 2012) 69.

Reference list

Articles/books/reports

Bendix, Reinhard, *Max Weber: An Intellectual Portrait* (University California Press, 1977)

Bennett, Jane, *The Enchantment of Modern Life: Attachments, Crossings, and Ethics* (Princeton University Press, 2001)

Berman, Harold, 'Some False Premises of Max Weber's Sociology of Law' (1987) 65 *Washington University Law Quarterly* 758

Blau, Peter, *Bureaucracy in Modern Society* (Random House, 1968)

Bolton, Sharon, *Emotion Management in the Workplace* (Palgrave Macmillan, 2004)

Boucock, Cary, *In the Grip of Freedom: Law and Modernity in Max Weber* (University of Toronto Press, 2000)

Clegg, Stewart, Martin Harris and Harro Hopfl, *Managing Modernity: Beyond Bureaucracy* (Oxford University Press, 2011)

Clegg, Stewart, *Modern Organisations: Organisation Studies in the Postmodern World* (Sage Publications, 1990)

Davidow William and Michael Malone, *The Virtual Corporation: Structuring and Revitalizing the Corporation for the 21st Century* (Harper, 1992)

Ewing, Sally, 'Formal Justice and the Spirit of Capitalism: Max Weber's Sociology of Law, (1987) 21(3) *Law and Society Review* 488

Feldman, Stephan, 'An Interpretation of Max Weber's Theory of Law: Metaphysics, Economics and the Iron Cage of Constitutional Law' (1991) *Law and Social Inquiry* 205

Goodin, Robert and Hans-Dieter Klingemann, *A New Handbook of Political Science in the Foundations of Bureaucracy in Economic and Social Thought* (Oxford University Press, 1996)

Gouldner, Alvin, *Patterns of Industrial Democracy* (Free Press, 1954)

Hecksher, Charles, 'Defining the Post Bureaucratic Type' in Charles Heckscher and Anne Donnellon (eds), *The Post Bureaucratic Organisation* (Sage Publications, 1994)

Hedland, Gunnar, 'The Hypermodern MNC: A Heterarchy?' (1986) 25(1) *Human Resource Management Journal* 9

Hennis, William, 'Max Weber's "Central Question"' (1983) 12(2) *Economy and Society* 135

Jenkins, Bill and Edward Page, *The Foundations of Bureaucracy in Economic and Social Thought II* (Edward Elgar Publishing, 2005)

Jewell, Chris, *Agents of the Welfare State: How Caseworkers Respond to Need in the United States, Germany and Sweden* (Palgrave MacMillan, 2007)

Kalberg, Stephen, 'Max Weber's Types of Rationality: Cornerstones for the Analysis of Rationalization Processes in History' (1980) 85(5) *American Journal of Sociology* 1145

Kolegar, Ferdinand, 'The Concept of "rationalization" and Cultural Pessimism in Max Weber's Sociology' (2005) 5(4) *Sociological Quarterly* 355

Kronman, Antony, *Max Weber* (Edward Arnold, 1983)

Krygier, Martin, *Ideals in the World* (Stanford University Press, 2012) 69

Lash, Scott and Sam Whimster, *Max Weber, Rationality and Modernity* (Allen & Unwin, 1987)

Levine, Donald, 'Rationality and Freedom: Weber and Beyond' (1981) 51(1) *Sociological Inquiry* 5

Löwith, Karl *Max Weber and Karl Marx* (Allen & Unwin, 1982)

Mashaw, Jerry, *Bureaucratic Justice* (Yale University Press, 1983)

Maynard-Moody, Steven and Michael Musheno, *Cops, Teachers, Councillors: Stories from the Front Line of Public Service* (University of Michigan Press, 2003)

Merton, Robert, *Bureaucratic Structure and Personality* (Free Press, 1957)

Milovanovic, Dragan, *Weberian and Marxist Analysis of Law* (Avebury, 1989)

Mintzberg, Henry, *Power in and Around Organisations* (Prentice-Hall, 1983)

Nonet, Phillippe, *Administrative Justice* (Russell Sage Foundation, 1969)

Nonet, Phillippe and Philip Selznick, *Law and Society in Transition: Toward Responsive Law* (Harper, 1978)

Ouchi, William, 'Markets, Bureaucracies and Clans' (1980) 25 *Administrative Science Quarterly* 129

Schluchter, Wolfgang, *The Rise of Western Rationalism: Max Weber's Developmental History* (University of California Press, 1981)

Selznick, Phillip, *Leadership in Administration* (University of California Press, 1957)

Sterling, Joyce and Wilbert Moore, 'Weber's Analysis of Legal Rationalisation: A Critique and Constructive Modification' (1987) 2(1) *Sociological Forum* 667

Trubek, David, 'Max Weber on Law and the Rise of Capitalism' (1972) *Wisconsin Law Review* 720

Weber, Max, *Economy and Society* (Harvard University Press, 1978)

Weber, Max, *The Methodology of the Social Sciences* (E A Shils and H A Finch trans and ed, Free Press, 2011) 578 [originally published 1949]

2 Contemporary public administration

The diffuse markers of responsive legality

Introduction

This chapter introduces the broad evidentiary basis of the overall responsive legality framework. It does this first through exploring contemporary public administration studies ranging across a number of law and social theory sub-disciplines to identify the real-world markers of responsive legality and, second, through introducing the framework of the RRT as the illustrative empirical site. Whilst Chapters 3, 4, 5 and 6 provide a detailed examination of responsive legality's component conceptual features, the goal of this chapter is more general: to make clear how the overall insights in the public administration studies might be more holistically accounted for in this framework of twenty-first-century justice.

In approaching this discussion, we might be mindful from the outset that various studies and scholars present divergent attitudes regarding the extent to which contemporary administration presents a break from earlier forms of governance. To some, not much has changed – any alleged 'changes' are merely reiterations of what has gone before.[1] Whilst this chapter aims to represent this difference of opinion by capturing perspectives that fall on both sides of the fence, we might still pause to reflect on the ramifications of this division for forming a broader theory of twenty-first-century justice.

Recall that the twentieth-century models of administrative justice presented in the previous chapter are ideal types. They are meant to represent general tendencies and clusters of ideas rather than actually existing states. From that perspective, the relevance of the question of whether contemporary public administration is fundamentally different from what has gone before is whether the nature of public administration has so fundamentally changed as to render these twentieth-century types incapable of capturing modern trends in public administration. As it is apparent from a range of interdisciplinary studies that the institutional logics of contemporary public administration have in some significant senses changed (senses caught under the diverse features of responsive legality) we might, of course, expect that the traditional theoretical models of administrative justice need to be supplemented. Even more recent models, such as those developed to explore mid-1980s' movements in public administration, also require updating to take account of these recent trends.

The first part of this discussion explores this literature, attempting to preserve the nuance regarding the views on its newness as far as possible. The second part of the discussion draws the general features together to explain where they might fit alongside twentieth-century models of administrative justice and to pave the way for the detailed consideration of the component features of the responsive-legality type.

Twenty-first-century public administration

As briefly noted already, one body of recent public administration work argues that contemporary administration is not radically different from what has gone before.[2] This might be thought of as a more moderate approach to conceptualising the sociological changes that have taken place for organisations in postmodernity, where scholars generally posit that there have been post-1980s' changes in the degree of hierarchy, authority and rationality that exist in public organisations but that these are, ultimately, of varying, and at times limited, degrees.

Harro Hopfl epitomises this view, arguing that contemporary organisations raise the same old issues of accountability as the traditional bureaucratic forms of administration.[3] He suggests that contemporary, or 'post-bureaucratic', organisations are characterised by teamwork, task groups, role flexibility, outsourcing, offshoring, dispensing with command and obedience relations and hierarchies, virtuality, networks, targets, entrepreneurship and self-motivation, cost units and the public sector by value for money. He also argues that contemporary and traditional, or 'bureaucratic' and 'post-bureaucratic', governance alike require trust in politicians, or bureaucrats, or both. Because there are no systems that guarantee that bureaucracy will be incorrupt and efficient or impersonal and objective, no accountability schema can immunise bureaucracy or contemporary forms of public administration against careerism and cynicism. In this way, concepts of bureaucracy and post-bureaucracy are effectively assimilated.

Jannis Kallinkos considers the way that new forms of communication and technology shape social production, in turn partially altering the bureaucratic form.[4] He argues that the traditional modernist bureaucracy is characterised by the contractual basis of individual participation in the organisation, where individuals join organisations in modern times on terms that are negotiable, concern specific contributions or functions and are revocable. However, he identifies a general trend in recent years away from this contractually based structure and towards open, fluid and shifting internet-based groups that have altered the social landscape in which organisations operate. There is a degree of nuance in Kallinkos's account in the sense that he concludes that although 'there are plenty of signs suggesting that these changes are far from transient and episodic and, crucially, indicative of wider shifts that betray a drift away from formal organisation (bureaucracy) as the dominant organisational template in modernity' (Clegg, 2011) the degree to which the contractually based bureaucratic organisational structure is seriously challenged by the trends associated with social production remains an 'open question'.

Stephen Ackroyd is more sceptical again of the notion that there has been a shift to entirely new forms of organisation, tracing the patterns of organisation across the UK manufacturing industry to show that two alleged features of contemporary public administration – fragmentation and disaggregation – are, in fact, long-standing features of British industrial organisation.[5] He posits that many large 'supposedly bureaucratic' manufacturing firms lacked the centralised direction and unitary structures that are part of classical models of bureaucracy, where they were often amalgamations of former competitors messily incorporated into one body. He then argues that the extent to which large British firms have been bureaucratically organised has been exaggerated and that not only is the concept of post-bureaucracy not applicable to the British manufacturing industry, but in fact, concepts of bureaucracy have also been misleading.[6] In this discussion, Ackroyd essentially encourages a retreat from large aggrandising conceptions of bureaucracy and post-bureaucracy (otherwise conceptualised as traditional versus contemporary forms of governance), instead encouraging a micro-focused analysis of each unit of particular organisations, as well as a consideration of the values that infuse organisational management as avenues for extracting important information about varying institutional landscapes.

Also sceptical of the notion that contemporary public administration is distinctly different from what has gone before, Mats Alvesson and Stanley Deetz posit that traditional notions of bureaucracy are still a dominant organisational form in contemporary society.[7] They argue in particular that there has been an increasing scholarly consideration of postmodern and critical approaches to organisation studies, seen, for example, in the development of Critical Management Studies conferences and the establishment of Critical Management Studies as an interest group within the Academy of Management. They suggest that the future enterprise of critical approaches to bureaucracy might involve considering organisational issues from an organisational participant's point of view, including appreciating the legitimacy of managerial viewpoints, rather than attempting to conceptually distinguish modern from postmodern forms of organisation. The normative socio-legal administrative justice sub-field is also aligned with this pursuit, and Adler's managerial model embodies many of the features discussed in this literature.[8]

In a similar vein, Paul Hoggett argues that whilst there have been new elements to organisational structure in the UK and elsewhere from the 1990s onwards, these changes should not be overestimated. He alleges that there has been a shift towards the creation of operationally decentralised units with a concurrent attempt to increase centralised control over strategy and policy.[9] Furthermore, he argues that the principle of competition has become the dominant method of organising these units and that during the most recent period there has been a significant development of processes of performance monitoring and management (involving inspections, audits, reviews and quality assessments), which is again oriented towards operationally decentralised units. He argues that whilst these indeed present a degree of variation on the pure bureaucratic form, 'they do not describe a simple movement from a bureaucratic to a post-bureaucratic form; rather, they combine strong elements of innovation with the reassertion of a number of fundamentally bureaucratic mechanisms' (Hoggett, 1996).

In contrast to these views on the moderate division between contemporary and more traditional forms of administration are those who argue that there is, in fact, a significant distinction between the two.

Charles Heckscher, for example, argues that contemporary organisations are characterised by 'interactive' systems of organisation, where everyone takes responsibility for the whole rather than for a particular job only.[10] For Heckscher, this system of interactive organisation is not a real system but an ideal type, in Weber's sense; one that organises reality 'by drawing, through the innumerable variations of real life, the boundaries where the terrain changes'.[11] These patterns are both logically and empirically deduced in Heckscher's study: logically in that they are patterns that 'make sense' and empirically in the sense that one can observe tendencies of these new elements that mix poorly with pre-existing bureaucratic structures to cause conflict around the edges. In this sense, Heckscher's approach has some affinity with the broad theoretical approach adopted in this book.

Heckscher observes that if one introduces a few bureaucratic elements into a communal organisation, the elements will either be rejected as 'foreign' or will have an impact on the organisation to such an extent that other aspects of it will also change until the entire system more closely resembles the bureaucratic model. For Heckscher, a high degree of conflict, excitement and unanticipated change in many companies provides an initial indication that we are seeing a new contemporary organisational post-bureaucratic *type*, distinct from traditional bureaucracy. This suspicion is reinforced as we see changes 'ripple out' to affect institutions far from the source and this new interactive type relies on a system of informed consensus rather than a hierarchy of authority. For Heckscher, there are 12 main trends that distinguish a bureaucracy from a post-bureaucracy or the contemporary organisation from the traditional organisation. First, whilst bureaucracies created consensus through acquiescence to authority, rules or traditions, the post-bureaucratic form creates these through institutionalised dialogue. Furthermore, dialogue is defined by the use of influence rather than power: in other words, people approach decision making based on their ability to persuade rather than their ability to command. In addition, influence in the contemporary organisation depends initially on trust; it depends on the belief that others are seeking mutual benefit rather than maximising gain. Fourth, there is a strong emphasis on organisational mission, where employees need to understand the key objectives in depth in order to coordinate their actions intelligently 'on the fly' or with a kind of initiative and goal-oriented efficiency. Fifth, in order for individuals to contribute to the mission, there is widespread sharing of information about corporate strategy. Sixth, the focus on mission must be supplemented by guidelines for action, which take the form of principles rather than rigid rules. Seventh, decision-making processes are fluid and must be frequently reconstructed; they cannot be directly 'read' from an organisational chart.

Eighth, managers in systems moving towards a more interactive form of organisation report a sense of loneliness and isolation in comparison to the 'old days' of professional bureaucracy, flowing from the fact that information systems have facilitated the building of temporary networks. Ninth, there must be an unusually thorough and open process of association and peer evaluation. Tenth, the system is relatively open at the boundaries, including in terms of career paths and the declining expectation in particular that employees will spend their entire careers in one organisation. Eleventh, there is an effort to reduce rules governing the treatment of employees and to minimise the element of personal judgement that was prevalent in bureaucracy, instead recognising a variety of individual performances based on the unique and specialist skills of each individual. And finally, there is an expectation of constant change in contrast to a bureaucratic expectation that decisions are made with a sense of 'permanence' in mind, because 'this is the right way of doing things'. In highlighting these differences, Heckscher concludes that although this ideal type may not yet exist in widespread empirical reality, these trends are reasonable, intuitive and logical projections that have begun to surface in particular areas of governance and that may provide greater understanding of an outline of the destinations of organisations and governmental structures in the future.

Paul Du Gay considers how problems of involvement and attachment, as characteristic human qualities, complicate organisational needs in bureaucratic and post-bureaucratic public management alike but nonetheless considers that there is a distinction between these two modes.[12] He considers the role of enthusiasm and responsiveness in the emotionally charged contemporary organisation, identifying that there has been an emphasis on breaking with bureaucratic norms and modes of conduct for the sake of innovation, risk taking and organisational and personal liberation. He argues, however, that this increased responsiveness and enthusiasm should be treated with scepticism because the demand for increased levels of personal involvement in policy application by career civil servants may compromise the institutional and ethical integrity of government.

In Du Gay's view, there has indeed been a shift towards greater personal involvement in government, and this has had the effect of undermining the important role played by the bureaucratic ethos and its spirit of formalistic impersonality in supporting the responsible operation of the state.

Stewart Clegg argues that 'modern bureaucracies are under reconstruction'[13] and that these reconstructions are to be defined in terms of new hybrid forms of organisation. According to Clegg, to understand modern organisations we need to view them through a dialectical lens, which reveals organisations as simultaneously decomposing and recomposing. Decomposition involves processes of supply chains and outsourcing (epitomised in the phenomenon of the call centre), which involve politics of surveillance and control. Recomposition, on the other hand, involves a range of new organisational dynamics characterised by the use of influence and persuasion rather than power exercised through command and control. In this new environment of influence and persuasion, leadership is not exercised through complex systems of rules but via guidelines for action, which take the form of broad and abstract principles 'expressing the reasons behind the rules'.[14] Within this new system of organisation, the decision-making power of the official is not derived from official rank but from the nature of the unique institutional problems at hand and the individual's capacity to solve those problems.

Similarly noting a marked shift in contemporary organisational structure, Guy Peters and Vincent Wright argue that, as outlined in the introduction to this book: 'of all areas of political science, no other has undergone a transformation comparable to that experienced by public administration over the past twenty years'.[15] They argue that this change has occurred to such an extent that 'all of the essential truths that guided practising public administrators and students of administration have now been challenged and often replaced'.[16] Whilst Peters and Wright argue that these profound changes are partially reflective of changes in concrete social practices, they also attribute them to changed scholarly attitudes towards these empirical changes, where new theoretical approaches have tended to emphasise the significant extent to which public administration is a political activity. According to Peters and Wright, these then, in turn, produce further changes for public administration.

One such new trend that they go on to discuss is the trend towards 'new managerialism',[17] where management ideas justified in the name of the three Es – economy, efficiency and effectiveness – have had profound effects on contemporary administration, primarily in the sense that the role of the public servant has become to run an organisation more efficiently, rather than participating in policy decisions. Although, as Halliday points out in his narrower critique of the socio-legal models of administrative justice, the persisting governmental emphasis on efficiency may not be too different from Mashaw's bureaucratic rationality[18] – Weber's bureaucratic form.[19]

Peters and Wright go on to point out that there is also what has been coined a 'new patrimonialism' associated with this new managerialism, whereby political leaders attempt to gain greater control over appointments to public office and at the same time extract greater loyalty from civil servants – a trend evident especially in the US, where a number of positions in the senior executive service have been opened to political appointment. Again associated with these changes, Peters and Wright identify a 'new fragmentation' of government and administration that they say has occurred in most political systems, with central governments decentralising and transferring more power to sub-national state officials or elected officials. They identify that these changes are producing a much less coherent framework for governance in most industrialised democracies, where the changes are typically justified in terms of efficiency. They go on to discuss that these recent trends of new managerialism, new patrimonialism and new fragmentation have had revolutionary effects to the point that the 'six great truths' about public administration have now been amended.

First, the idea that public administration needs to be self-sufficient has been challenged by the interconnected policies of sub-contracting, privatisation and competition. Second, older ideas about hierarchical management in bureaucracy are now being reassessed in the light of ideas about 'empowerment', involving the granting of increased organisational power to both employees and clients of public organisations. Within this new ideology, lower-level government employees are to be empowered and given more control over their own jobs so that they can make their own decisions and be held accountable for them. Third, they identify that the traditional assumption in public administration that all citizens should receive equal benefits from the state and bear equal burden to support the state (partially justified through the creation of large centralised bureaucracies in modern states, especially the welfare states of Europe, where training, rules and supervision were used to produce equality) has been replaced by alternative models. Under these alternative models, decentralisation and deconcentration of administration have become 'popular antidotes for the alleged failings of centralisation'.[20]

Furthermore, the spread of partially autonomous agencies, the introduction of markets, and the delegation of implementation to third-sector bodies have combined to 'blur the traditional lines of responsibility'.[21] In this context, a new principle of accountability downwards has emerged where innovations such as the naming of public officials under the introduction of publicised quality and performance indicators alter traditional hierarchical structures. In addition, there has been a rejection of former standardised employment procedures, where individuals are now rewarded according to their merits rather than their particular rank in the system.

Finally, Peters and Wright outline that the assumption that the public service is, can be and should be politically neutral has been called into question. There is now a trend towards the politicisation of administration in many developed countries, where civil servants are increasingly being told that they should be aggressive and entrepreneurial in pursuing the goals of their organisations. They conclude that, whilst the shift from old public administration to New Public Management has varied in timing, pace and intensity across developed countries, such changes have nonetheless widely taken place and have seen a new list of governance 'principles' being generated to accord with the political thinking of the day.

Sharon Bolton also documents changes to the contemporary organisation, outlining that over the past 20 years orthodox accounts of the organisation as a formal structure populated by rational office holders have been displaced with the finding that organisations as clusters of human individuals have feelings and that organisational actors regularly utilise emotions in the course of their work.[22] She argues that, whereas for much of the last century emotions were assigned to an 'unanalysed motivational reservoir', employees' 'sentiments' have now become a central focus of analysis.[23]

Bolton notes that for early management writers, epitomised by Weber and his work on bureaucratic impersonality and the 'little cog' of the machine-like worker,[24] the bureaucratic personality is the only permissible kind, and if maximum efficiency is to be achieved then 'emotion definitely cannot be written into an organisational actor's script'.[25]

New management theory, however, represents a clear break from these traditional notions, recognising that the design of work is of course influenced on a day-to-day basis by the many social interactions of individuals and that the individual 'can find ingenious ways to circumvent the formal structure of an organisation'.[26] Bolton concludes that the labour market is increasingly focused on creativity, rather than rule-bound behaviour and that communication, teamwork, customer care, individual initiative and self-reliance are seen as new key skills.

In dialogue with these changes, Steven Maynard-Moody and Michael Musheno observe the increasingly dynamic, nonprocedural characteristics of contemporary officials, often noting that these organic values perform a more personalised role in governance than was the case for the traditional bureaucrat. They emphasise the shifting subjectivity of contemporary street-level bureaucrats, finding that their research subjects – police officers, teachers and councillors – first make their own judgements about offenders, children and clients and then apply, mould or abandon rules and procedures to support these attitudes.[27] In the words of one of their schoolteacher participants,

> I deal with the kids one to one, whereas the administration deals with the kids as a whole. [The administrators] have to look at what is good for the building as a whole, meaning the 623 students we have here. I look at it on a case-by-case, class-by-class basis. [The administrators] are consistently telling me I have to look at it the other way, and I never will because I deal with the personalities, the faces, the parents, and the problems on a one-to-one basis, and sometimes what's good for a kid is not what's good as a general principle for the entire building or another school. I look at it on a kid-by-kid basis. I really don't care what the building policy is.[28]

Importing the public administration literature into the socio-legal models

Whilst there is evidently variation in the extent to which public administration scholars believe that there is something new about contemporary organisations, the crucial task when it comes to considering applicably related frameworks of administrative justice is that we consider where – new or not – the core elements explored across the wider public administration literature are adequately reflected in the twentieth-century models. Whilst many of the component features discussed earlier are importantly reflected in Adler's managerial, consumer and market types (though, as suggested, managerial and market might be bracketed off here for their conceptual perpetuation of Mashaw's bureaucratic rationality), there are a number of persisting analytical features that we might additionally import into these models to capture the complexity of the ideal-typical form of twenty-first-century administrative justice.

As the ideal-typical methodology encourages, we need not treat the aforementioned literature as presenting narrow concrete iterations or 'lists' of features or terms that should somehow be accounted for in assessing contemporary manifestations of administrative justice. It is not that there are five or six bullet points of factors that the leading administrative justice models do not account for. Rather, when we are sensitive to the generalised patterns that this literature documents, it becomes clear that there is a pervasive degree of generalised creativity, innovation, emotionality, adaptability, fluidity, complexity, differentiation and malleability – which manifests in a wide array of forms across public organisations – that is not captured in twentieth-century conceptions of administrative justice.

In exploring these elements further, the subsequent Chapters 4, 5, 6 and 7 hone in on each feature to illuminate how aspects of these diffuse and generalised elements are embodied in the responsive-legality type.

For now, the second half of this chapter considers the empirical fieldwork site that is drawn on to *illustrate* the component features of responsive legality.

The fieldwork site: the Refugee Review Tribunal of Australia

Introduction

As outlined in the introductory chapter, the empirical dimension of the research for this book was confined to the Refugee Review Tribunal of Australia (RRT). Whilst there were many iterations and reiterations of the research design, the research questions and the rationales behind them,[29] the data collected in the end played a background or supporting role to illustrate the features of the ideal type discerned analytically from the broader literature.

The process of collecting, interpreting and analysing this material, as well as considerations of the data's generalisability and limitations, are presented briefly – to not distract from the substantive findings and argument – in the final part of this chapter. The discussion of the interview material itself, alongside the core features of responsive legality that they illuminate, is contained in Chapters 3, 4, and 5. The first part of this RRT-related discussion provides a descriptive background to the operations of the RRT and its place within Australian public administration and a brief and condensed discussion of the reasons why in the end the RRT proved to be a serendipitous site for illuminating the responsive-legality ideal type. The second part of the discussion briefly examines the empirical methodology employed to invite readers to scrutinise the validity and reliability of the interview data.

Background to the RRT

The officials who participated in the research were former members of the RRT; 40 semi-structured interviews were conducted with former members of the RRT who voluntarily and anonymously participated in the research.

At the date that the research for this book commenced, the RRT was jointly operated with the Migration Review Tribunal (MRT). However, on 1 July 2015, after the interviews had already been conducted and analysed, the RRT was amalgamated with the Administrative Appeals Tribunal (AAT)[30] – a nationwide Australian tribunal responsible for reviewing administrative decisions made under more than 400 acts of the Commonwealth Parliament.[31] Since this date, the former RRT has been operating as the Refugee and Migration Division of the AAT. Whilst some of the former RRT procedures have been altered since its amalgamation with the AAT to reflect changes in legislation and to streamline the procedure, the majority of procedures and practices remain the same as they did under the RRT.[32]

Regardless of these procedural changes, the interviews with former RRT members remain rich resources for administrative justice theory building. Were the book intent on unearthing actual objective information about the way the tribunal was organised or run, or were it motivated towards producing particular policy outcomes, these changes in procedure would – depending on the precise nature of the question asked – potentially alter the relevance of this study's findings. However, learning more about public officials' and organisations' normative justificatory logics did not require any particular institutional formation as a prerequisite for extrapolating relevant and reliable findings. Therefore, the remainder of this chapter discusses the composition of the RRT (as it then was) before 1 July 2015 for the purposes of placing the interview material in its appropriate empirical context, bearing in mind that subsequent institutional changes have little effect on the study's overall findings.

Salient features of RRT decision making

The RRT is an appeal-level government body, initially established in 1993, in which members hear appeals from unsuccessful refugee protection decisions made by front-line Department of Immigration and Border Protection (DIABP) officials.[33] Its functions are laid out in Part 7 of the *Migration Act 1958* (Cth)[34] and the *Migration Regulations 1994* (Cth),[35] which implement Australia's protection obligations to refugees under the *Convention Relating to the Status of Refugees*[36] into Australian law. In conducting the refugee protection visa assessment, the primary obligation is to

> [n]ot return a person in any manner whatsoever to the frontiers of territories where the person's life or freedom would be threatened on account of his or her race, religion, nationality, membership of a particular social group or political opinion.[37]

Many of the tribunal's practice notes and guidelines exist to give effect to this obligation.[38] Members of the RRT are charged with reviewing the primary DIABP delegate's decision, with the power to affirm the primary decision and make a new decision or return the matter to the DIABP with directions for reconsideration.[39] In doing so, they may exercise all of the powers and discretions conferred on the primary decision maker within the same legislative framework.[40] The RRT is constituted by a single member solely responsible for making the decision, but with the potential for assistance by a Legal Section Unit made up of internal staff providing legal advice to members and the option of being assisted by the informal advice of senior staff and colleagues.[41]

Applicants who are unsuccessful in the RRT can seek judicial review through the courts in limited cases,[42] where their decision may be reviewed and returned to the RRT if it is found that there was an error of law.[43] Furthermore, when the applicant is unsuccessful in the RRT, the Minister for Immigration and Border Protection may personally consider and grant a visa on humanitarian grounds if he or she considers it to be in the public interest.[44]

In reviewing refugee protection applications, the RRT does not function as a court. A federal-level 'court' has a technical constitutional meaning under Australian law in that it is a body established under Chapter III of the *Australian Constitution* and its predominant function is to exercise federal judicial power.[45] The *Australian Constitution* designates a formal separation of powers, conferring legislative power on the federal legislature under Chapter I, executive power on the federal executive under Chapter II and judicial power on the federal judiciary under Chapter III. The RRT – as with all other Australian government tribunals – belongs to the executive branch of government, and therefore, its members carry out executive rather than judicial functions.

This, on the face of it, is different from the official role of a tribunal in many other legal systems; for instance, it is different from the UK system, which does not embody a formal separation of powers and therefore does not formally distinguish between judicial and non-judicial power.[46] Whilst the US system acknowledges a formal separation of powers, it does not require such a sharp distinction between judicial and non-judicial functions as in Australia. Put another way, the role of US 'administrative judges' constitutes somewhat of a middle ground between Australian tribunal 'members' and UK tribunal 'judges'.[47] This translates into some jurisdictional differences between Australian tribunal members and UK Asylum Immigration Tribunal (AIT) 'judges', for example, in that, unlike in the Australian RRT context, the AIT may not – even in theory – consider the merits of the policy. It is only if a policy is in 'absolute terms' that leave the decision maker with no discretion, or where

> on the facts of the case there is no proper opportunity, by application of the policy, to make a decision unfavourable to the applicant, that the AIT can allow an appeal on the basis of non-application or misapplication of the policy.[48]

However, the distinction between tribunals and courts is recognised and clearly drawn even in systems that lack a clear separation of powers; at least since the establishment of the separation of powers in the eighteenth century, the judicial branch has typically been associated with superior central courts that can be easily contrasted with inferior and local tribunals. The critical point here is that the RRT, whilst technically occupying a distinctly Australian legal landscape by virtue of its constitutional separation of powers, may in essence share much in common even with those tribunals that are not technically regulated by the same separation of powers requirements. In this similarity, it might provide a level of generalisability for thinking about tribunal operations reaching beyond the Australian context.

Matters reviewed by the RRT

The core function of the RRT is to review appeals from unsuccessful primary-level refugee protection visa applications. To be successful, the applicant must satisfy the definition of *refugee* under the *Refugee Convention*, which defines a refugee as a person who

> [o]wing to a well-founded fear of being persecuted for reasons of race, religion, nationality, membership of a particular social group or political opinion, is outside the country of his nationality and is unable, or, owing to such fear, is unwilling to avail himself of the protection of that country; or who, not having a nationality and being outside the country of his former habitual residence, is unable, or, owing to such fear, is unwilling to return to it.[49]

The refugee definition evidently includes a number of elements, including that: the applicant has 'a well-founded fear of being persecuted'; the persecution feared by the applicant is 'for reasons of race, religion, nationality, membership of a particular social group or political opinion' (commonly referred to as persecution for 'a Convention reason'); the applicant is 'outside the country of his nationality' or has no nationality; and the applicant is unable or unwilling to avail himself or herself of the protection of the country of his or her nationality (or, if he has no nationality, the country of his former habitual residence).

A number of provisions of the *Migration Act* expressly qualify Australia's implementation of certain aspects of the *Refugee Convention*, focusing especially on concepts of persecution and the nature and seriousness of certain crimes relevant to the determination of whether Australia has protection obligations to an asylum seeker. The term *persecuted* in Article 1A(2) is qualified by s 91R(1) of the *Migration Act*, which provides that Article 1A(2) does not apply unless persecution for one or more of the *Refugee Convention* reasons is the 'essential and significant reason(s), for the persecution'; the persecution involves 'serious harm' to the person; and the persecution involves 'systematic and discriminatory conduct'. Section 91R(2) of the *Migration Act* provides a non-exhaustive list of instances of 'serious harm', including a threat to the person's life or liberty, significant physical harassment of the person, significant physical ill treatment of the person, significant economic hardship that threatens the person's capacity to subsist and denial of capacity to earn a livelihood of any kind, in situations when the denial threatens the person's capacity to subsist.[50]

Since the introduction of what is known as the 'complementary protection regime' in 2013, the ambit of the RRT's functions has widened to grant protection to an applicant for whom

> [t]here are substantial grounds for believing that, as a necessary and foreseeable consequence of a person being removed from Australia to a receiving country, there is a real risk that he or she will suffer significant harm.[51]

Whilst these changes are of minimal relevance to this book – inasmuch as the tribunal members interviewed were all former members sitting on the RRT before the complementary protection regime was introduced – the members did at times reflect on the regime in their discussions of tribunal decision making,[52] thus making it contextually relevant to the later analysis of interview data.

Aside from the legal framework, tribunal decision making is also guided by a number of policy and procedural manuals and guidance notes. These include practice guidelines on gender-related claims, guidance notes on the assessment of applicant credibility, guidance on how to deal with vulnerable persons, and guidance on expert opinion evidence. In addition to these subject-specific guidelines, there are a range of varying ministerial guidelines and principal member directions available to members. These include ministerial directions on applicant processing priorities to determine the order of priority for hearing various forms of claims, principal member directions designating the constitution of the tribunal and further delineating priorities for allocating and processing cases, member directions on the management of cases of persons in immigration detention, member directions on the efficient conduct of reviews, directions on putting adverse information orally to applicants, guidelines on the referral of cases to the Minister for Immigration for special 'intervention into the matter', guidelines with regards to the handling of privacy breaches, guidelines in relation to costs arising from applications for review and guidelines in relation to oaths and affirmations. Members are also guided by a Procedures Advice Manual (PAM), which provides comprehensive information regarding the procedural regime governing their decision making. Whilst these guidelines themselves are not legally binding on tribunal members, most of their substantive content derives from the *Migration Act* and *Migration Regulations*, such that their substance is effectively binding on members by virtue of its derivation from legislation.

Tribunal members are also provided with a range of information regarding the country situation of applicants, called Country Information (CI) reports, to provide factual content to assist in making their determination. These reports come in a variety of forms, produced from varying sources and organisations. The RRT itself has a research unit responsible for internally producing CI reports, and members are also able to access CI documents collated by a number of bodies, including human rights organisations such as Amnesty International and government departments such as the Department of Foreign Affairs.

Merits review

By virtue of the RRT's status as a tribunal within the executive branch of government, RRT members are required to make an administrative reconsideration of a case based on the facts rather than a judicial reconsideration of the case based on the law. They are charged with assessing the factual merits of a decision rather than its legal correctness – although the extent to which these two things can be clearly separated has been a matter of debate.[53]

The principal objective of merits review is to ensure that the correct or preferable decision is reached in the particular case.[54] When considering whether a decision is 'correct or preferable', Brennan J (the first president of the Administrative Appeals Tribunal) commented that

> [a]lthough the tribunal is, and a court is not, concerned with [the] merits of a reviewable decision which do not affect the validity of the decision, both are concerned to inquire whether the decision was made within the powers vested by the decision maker. There is no dichotomy between the administrative standards upon which the tribunal must insist and by which its decisions are made effective, and the principles of law which are applied by a court: administrative action which exceeds the power conferred is not only ineffective in point of law, but it constitutes unacceptable administrative conduct.[55]

The difference between merits review and judicial review is summed up in the Report of the Commonwealth Administrative Review Committee (Kerr Committee Report) 1971. There, the committee argued that because the vast majority of administrative decisions involve the exercise of discretion on non-justiciable grounds, reviewing the merits of these decisions is a non-judicial function.[56] However, there is some controversy surrounding this assertion, with administrative-law scholars arguing that the proposition that the vast majority of administrative decisions involve the exercise of discretion on non-justiciable grounds is highly questionable.[57]

These various interpretations have some significance when thinking about attitudes towards legality and justice in the RRT, as they reveal that there are reasonable variations in interpretation, from a doctrinal perspective, even in answering the basic technical question of how central the law actually is to RRT decision making. Whilst there are mixed views on this, it has been argued in line with the Kerr Committee Report that the substantive distinction between merits review and judicial review is 'artificial rather than functional' and 'productive of considerable practical problems'.[58] Whilst on one level merits review is based on a contrast between the 'legality' of the decision and the 'merits' of the decision made in the implementation of rules,[59] in reality the jurisdiction of merits review amalgamates both factual merits-based *and* legal questions. Indeed, the courts have found that whilst merits review bodies have the jurisdiction to review decisions 'on the merits', this is not all that they can do.[60] In addition to the non-judicial power of reviewing decisions on their merits, merits review tribunals can also exercise what Australian constitutional law sometimes refers to as an 'innominate function' – that is, a function that can be allocated to a judicial or a non-judicial body and assumes in a chameleon-like way the character of the body to which it is allocated: non-judicial if allocated to a non-judicial body and judicial if allocated to a judicial body.[61] The only limitation in deciding these questions of law is that the merits review body cannot decide legal questions 'conclusively' if the question relates to a 'controversy out of existing rights and duties'.[62] However, a further caveat to this distinction is that even the term *conclusively* has been a matter of debate. What is 'conclusive' or 'non-conclusive' has been framed both in terms of the distinction between appeal and judicial review (where a conclusive decision could be challenged according to an appeal whereas a non-conclusive decision could be challenged by way of judicial review or in 'collateral proceedings', such as proceedings to enforce a particular decision) and alternatively framed with regard to the distinction between void and voidable decisions.[63] Acknowledging these ambiguities in the scope of merits review, we might conclude that the substantive distinction between merits review and judicial review – the distinction between legality and merits – is considerably less significant than is commonly assumed,[64] giving RRT members a range of both legal and non-legal powers and duties.

The conduct of reviews

The RRT's procedures are designed to 'provide a review process that is fair, just, informal and quick and ensure that the applicant can fully put his or her case before the tribunal'.[65] The RRT explicitly aims to 'make the correct decision in individual cases and to influence decision making through quality and consistency of decisions'.[66]

The RRT's procedures are relatively informal, and hearings are conducted by a single member. The minister for immigration and border protection is not represented in any cases, and whilst the applicant may appoint a representative who is trained as a migration agent to assist with his or her case, this is often not pursued. In 2013–2014, as a recent example, this occurred in only approximately 30 per cent of cases. The hearings do not follow a strict procedure, although evidence is usually taken under oath or affirmation and hearings are closed to the public.

The RRT's policy is to review protection visa cases within 90 days of the receipt of the DIABP's documents regarding the decision. They aim to do this in 70 per cent of cases, recognising that a review within 90 days may not always be possible. This may not be possible where, for example, a backlog might prevent a standard being met, more than one hearing might be required, hearings may need to be rescheduled for reasons beyond the tribunal's control, the applicant may request further time to obtain evidence or make a submission, new information may become available or another body or agency may be required to provide a report or assessment. In pursuance of its core mandate to 'provide a review process that is fair, just, informal and quick', the RRT aims to conduct 'independent, expert review of migration and refugee decisions that is efficient and accessible'.[67]

In attempts to concretise this vision, the RRT has adopted a service charter. The charter outlines the RRT's commitment to providing a professional and courteous service to review applicants, claiming that following the service charter it seeks to satisfy a number of core expectations. These expectations include that RRT personnel will, for example, be polite, respectful, courteous and prompt in their dealings with applicants; use language that is clearly and easily understood; and abide by the Australian Public Service Values and Code of Conduct.[68]

In conducting protection visa reviews, the RRT processes an onerous caseload, with 6,863 cases lodged in the RRT as at 30 June 2014,[69] and all outstanding cases to be processed in the Refugee and Immigration Division.[70] Of the decided cases in 2014, 22 per cent of primary decisions were set aside, 72 per cent of primary decisions were affirmed and 6 per cent of cases were withdrawn or otherwise resolved. From January to 30 June 2014, 4,411 hearings were conducted, representing 80 per cent of matters. The average time taken to decide a matter in that year was 34 weeks, reflecting a lengthy process of the decision maker becoming familiar with the applicant's claims, conducting the hearing and, if necessary, a rehearing, and writing the decision. Over this time, interpreters were required 87 per cent of the time and between them spoke ninety-eight languages and dialects.

Of the RRT decisions made from January to 30 June 2014, 30.7 per cent were taken to the courts for judicial review. Of that percentage, only 0.8 per cent were set aside as a result of judicial review. This low overturn rate can at least partially be understood in the context of s 474(1) of the *Migration Act*,[71] which functions as a privative clause restricting access to courts for judicial review of administrative decisions made under the *Migration Act*. Section 474(1) states that

> [a] decision . . . made . . . under the *Migration Act* is final and conclusive;[72] must not be challenged, appealed against, reviewed, quashed, or called into question in any court;[73] and is not subject to prohibition, mandamus, injunction, declaration or certiorari in any court on any account.[74]

In interpreting s 474(1), the High Court has found that reference to 'a decision' is to a legally valid decision and that a purported decision made without jurisdiction is, as a matter of law, no decision at all.[75] As such, the privative clause does not prevent judicial review of purported decisions that are not, as a matter of law, decisions under the *Migration Act*. Whilst there is widespread judicial controversy over the practical scope and effect of this finding,[76] judicial attempts have been made to clarify the position on what precisely constitutes an error of law such that it will not be exempt from judicial review under s 474. In this clarification the court has distinguished between inferior courts, on one hand, and administrative decision makers and tribunals, on the other.[77] In lower courts, the class of errors amounting to jurisdictional error is narrower than the class that go to jurisdiction for administrative decision makers and tribunals. The majority in *Craig v South Australia* found that

> [a]t least in the absence of a contrary intent in the statute or other instrument which established it, an administrative tribunal lacks authority either to authoritatively determine questions of law or to make an order or decision otherwise than in accordance with the law . . . If such an administrative tribunal falls into an error of law which causes it to identify a wrong issue, to ask itself a wrong question, to ignore relevant material, to rely on irrelevant material or, at least in some circumstances, to make an erroneous finding

> or to reach a mistaken conclusion, and the tribunal's exercise or purported exercise of power is thereby affected, it exceeds its authority or powers. Such an error of law is jurisdictional error, which will invalidate any order or decision of the tribunal which reflects it.[78]

An error of law can thus be seen to include a number of different types of error, and there is a prima facie assumption that every error of substantive law committed by an administrative tribunal will be jurisdictional error, providing the error of law can be seen to have contributed to the decision reached by the tribunal.[79] This is based on the presumption that Parliament did not intend that the jurisdiction of an administrative tribunal should wrongly extend to determining questions of law or making decisions other than those that are in accordance with law.

The people

Appointments

Members of the RRT are appointed by the governor general through a merits-based recruitment process. The minister for immigration and border protection recommends to the cabinet that certain applicants be appointed. The cabinet then presents its recommendations to the governor general.[80] Members are then appointed by the governor general to statutory offices for fixed terms on a full- or part-time basis for up to five years. Together, today,[81] there are 137 tribunal members in twelve teams across Adelaide, Brisbane, Melbourne, Perth and Sydney.

The tribunal is managed by a principal member (PM) who is the 'executive officer' of the tribunal and is responsible for its overall operation and administration, including 'monitoring the operations to ensure that those operations are as fair, just, economical, informal and quick as practicable'.[82] The PM may give written directions regarding the operation of the tribunal and the conduct of reviews.[83] Senior management of the tribunal is also composed of a deputy principal member who is responsible for member performance and professional development under the guidance of the PM,[84] senior members who take an active role in guiding other members under the guidance of the PM, and registrars, deputy registrars and other officers of the tribunal who perform a range of duties and functions as the PM directs.

Members' qualifications

It is the tribunal's policy to continually review strategies to attract, retain and develop high-quality staff.[85] In its recruitment process, the tribunal engages a wide range of skills and expertise, from general administrative staff to lawyers, accountants, and human resource and technology professionals. Whilst there are no compulsory qualification requirements for the appointment of members, members appointed to the tribunal have typically had extensive senior-level experience in the private or public sector. They are appointed as generalists to country information rather than specialists in a particular area.[86]

Whilst statistics on the current number of members who are legally trained are not available, the latest available data reveal that in 2007–2008, 71 per cent of tribunal members held formal legal qualifications, whilst 29 per cent of tribunal members did not.[87] Of the former members interviewed who sat on the tribunal at various points over the past several years, 57 per cent of members were legally qualified,[88] and 43 per cent of members interviewed were not. Those interviewed with legal qualifications completed law degrees across a range of Australian universities and practised across a range of legal specialisations spanning commercial law, migration law, administrative law, family law and constitutional law, amongst other areas.[89] These individuals had practised in a number of contexts, including in private practice, public-service departments and international agencies and in roles as solicitors or barristers at different levels of seniority.[90] The interviewed members who had not practised law came from a diverse range of backgrounds, including journalism, international diplomacy, academia, nursing, psychology, international relations and linguistics.

Legally and non-legally trained members alike were typically high-performing individuals who had reached a certain level of experience and expertise in their career. They were generally highly skilled and of a relatively mature age and experience, enabling them to meet the requirements of a demanding position. This reflects the current composition of the RRT.[91] In 2014, for example, there were no members under the age of 25, two members between the ages of 25 and 34, 25 members between the ages of 35 and 44, 49 members between the ages of 45 and 54, 48 members between the ages of 55 and 64, and 13 members over 65 years of age.[92] The interviewed participants themselves commonly reflected on the maturity and experience required to fulfil the demanding role, with one member encapsulating this sentiment with the assertion that 'it is not a young person's game'.[93]

Under the tribunal Enterprise Agreement 2012–2014, there is a strong aim to support productivity improvement and initiatives, to recognise the participation of employees and to provide a positive work environment in the RRT.[94] Under the agreement, the tribunal aims to encourage employees and managers to prioritise workloads with reasonable working hours, maintain a strong performance-based culture, increase operational efficiency with streamlined administrative processes and working arrangements, recognise and value the participation of employees, attract and retain staff, provide a positive working environment, provide flexibility in working hours to assist employees balance their professional and personal lives, and uphold the Australian Public Service (APS) values.[95] RRT members are remunerated with an annual salary according to their rank within the APS, with salary advancement occurring through each classification when an employee is assessed as 'effective' or above in his or her performance appraisal.[96]

Overall, the RRT members interviewed, as with those on the tribunal over time more broadly, reflect a diverse range of professional, personal and cultural backgrounds, bringing a range of unique skills and approaches to their decision making.[97]

Reasons for field site selection

Socio-legal serendipity

On a messy and mundane level,[98] the RRT site was selected because access to conduct empirical research with past members was practically possible in this forum based on the authors' past work experience and professional networks. The process of speaking with former members of the tribunal was perhaps serendipitous,[99] as it allowed for the extrapolation of material in interviews that provided far more detail and insight into these officials' actual attitudes than undoubtedly would have been the case were the interview process controlled by the tribunal management. These limitations were acknowledged by the only researcher with published findings who has been granted official access to interview RRT members,[100] who lamented, in interview, the limited insights revealed by speaking to current members influenced by their own career concerns and fears about speaking out of turn and compromising their good standing with the tribunal.[101] The opportunity to speak to former members was a prime example of Simon Halliday and Patrick Schmidt's notion of the logics of proof, discovery, accuracy and explication being demarcated by a 'thin line of serendipity [that] cuts across and intervenes'[102] to enliven the research.

CONDUIT FOR STUDYING BUREAUCRATIC OFFICIALS' NORMATIVE LOGICS

To constitute an appropriate forum for evaluating bureaucratic normative logics in the construction of administrative justice frames, the chosen site, of course, must be composed of individuals that we can call 'bureaucrats'. To make this assessment we might refer back to Weber's well-known definition of government bureaucrats, where bureaucrats operating within public administration operate according to six core principles. According to Weber, bureaucracy involves a fixed and official jurisdictional area generally ordered by rules, laws or administrative regulations; it operates according to principles of office hierarchy and levels of graded authority where there is supervision of lower offices by higher offices; management of the office is based on written documents; it requires office management that presupposes thorough and expert training; when the office is fully developed, official activity requires the full working capacity of the official; and the management of the office follows general rules, which are more or less stable and involve jurisprudence or administrative or business management and which can be learnt.[103]

On a general level, the daily routine tasks of RRT members, in deciding refugee protection claims according to standardised criteria and legal and procedural guidelines,[104] in essence, reflects this procedural routinisation that Weber takes as definitional of bureaucracy. Whilst RRT members are typically highly educated and highly skilled in a manner not widely reflected across bureaucratic structures, and the emotional and psychological burdens on RRT members may be more heightened than in many other areas of government decision making, their role in reviewing the decision according to the same sets of rules and discretions as the primary decision maker is essentially procedural and standardised in nature, reflecting the core tenet of Weber's conception of bureaucracy. Weber's six core elements of bureaucracy are also generally reflected in RRT operations, though not to the exclusion of individual discretion. Generally speaking, decision makers are typically cognisant of administrative regulations,[105] operate according to principles of office hierarchy,[106] follow office rules delineated in written documents,[107] implement expert training,[108] work at full training capacity[109] and follow general rules of jurisprudence and administration.[110]

However, we might take note that – reflecting this combination of traditional and contemporary elements of bureaucracy – RRT decision making involves both standardised procedural elements that typify traditional modernist conceptions of bureaucracy, as well as more subjective and personalised bureaucratic behaviours, providing a conduit for further evaluations of contemporary bureaucracy. RRT members are afforded high amounts of discretion and are selected on the basis of their high levels of experience, qualifications and maturity – elements not necessary to perform highly within a modernist structure of bureaucracy, closely tied to basic mechanical routines. In this sense, the RRT presents an ideal site for extending understandings of contemporary public administration. It embodies a kind of organic complexity that extends beyond traditional conceptions of modernist bureaucracy to tell us more about the potential complexity of contemporary governance and administrative justice consciousness, which may be a reaction to the hybrid roles and functions often allocated to contemporary government officials,[111] such as those in the RRT.[112]

Further, the RRT was a serendipitously ideal site for filling some of the analytical gaps in the pre-existing socio-legal models of administrative justice. There are four interrelated reasons why this is the case. First, the RRT typifies a higher level of government not explored in the predominantly front-line (and occasionally appeal-level) contexts studied in the initial socio-legal models of administrative justice. For this reason, this study contributes to building a more complete picture of government administration through which the ideal types can be explored.

Second, composed as it is of a body of professional, educated, passionate, career-level civil servants, the RRT typifies many of the aspects of contemporary public administration discussed in the reviewed interdisciplinary public administration literature. Centring on this 'higher-level' public official, the RRT illustrates many emergent trends in twenty-first-century public administration discussed at length in the previous chapter. Generally summarised, these include greater levels of organisational innovation, higher levels of emotionality, increased fluidity and a more nuanced ability for officials to enact rules in pursuit of their contextual purpose.[113]

Third, the RRT's highly sensitive and politicised refugee jurisdiction – where so much is at stake in the lives of applicants, and this is of course known and understood by the expert administrators making decisions and applying their conceptions of administrative justice – provides a rich forum for the deep and detailed examination of a range of normative values motivating decision making, as reflected more broadly in the public administration literature. Consideration of a more technical jurisdiction – such as the Consumer, Trader and Tenancy Tribunal or the Motor Accidents Authority (both of which, incidentally, were considered but dismissed as potential research sites) – would ultimately not have unearthed some of the rich legitimating values that are more broadly noted as characterising recent movements in public administration.

Fourth, RRT officials reflect a combination of traditional and contemporary decision making traits such that the site reveals insights regarding the enduring features of governance debated in the related literature. In other words, in a number of senses, RRT decision making involves both standardised procedural elements that typify traditional modernist conceptions of public administration, as well as more subjective and personalised behaviours, providing a conduit for further evaluations of contemporary organisations more broadly. As discussed in the previous section, RRT members are afforded significant amounts of discretion and are selected on the basis of their high levels of experience, qualifications and maturity – elements not necessary to perform well within a modernist structure of bureaucracy, closely tied to basic mechanical routines. In this sense, the RRT presents a promising site for extending understandings of administrative justice in contemporary public administration, embodying a kind of complexity that extends beyond traditional structures of modernist bureaucracy to tell us more about the potential complexity of the normative logics of the more value driven contemporary official.

Amidst this blend of attractive reasons for selecting the RRT to study the normative logics that motivate administrative decision making we might be mindful of the site's basic limitations. The most obvious and basic concern is whether RRT officials are really generalisable subjects for thinking about government officials more broadly, when the bulk of administrative action takes place on the front line? Whilst this is an understandable question, the informed and important response, as the review of the socio-legal and public administration literature in Chapter 1 and this chapter attests, is that these features are becoming clearly evidenced across a range of public administration contexts at all levels of governance. This means that whilst the higher-level appeal jurisdiction studied here is likely to illuminate these features more clearly than many contexts would, it remains a rich embodiment site for these broader trends and an ideal illustrative context to draw together the divergent features of the emergent responsive-legality type.

As such, the investigation into the normative bases on which administrators justify their decisions in the RRT provides new insights into what motivates government officials in their daily decision making. The RRT has proved a fortunate and serendipitous site for socio-legal administrative-justice theory building, and - far more broadly - it has allowed for the discernment of rich conceptual relationships between public officials' motivating ideals and attitudes towards justice. In this, it empirically captures the culmination of newly complex value systems that drive contemporary public organisations forward.

Empirical research techniques

Introduction

The final part of this chapter discusses *briefly* (without distracting from the substantive findings and claims), the methodology that was employed in the empirical component of the study. It begins with a discussion of the core interview design, considering the interviews employed in terms of representativeness, and semi-structured questions. It then discusses the methods employed to analyse the interview transcripts and ensure optimum validity and reliability. In terms of validity, it discusses approaches employed to overcome 'the problem of anecdotalism'[114] through applications of triangulation, the refutability principle, the constant comparative method, comprehensive data treatment and deviant case analysis. It then discusses measures employed to ensure the reliability of results, considering the use of low-inference descriptors and the creation of clearly conceptualised constructs. Accordingly, the empirical component of this chapter proceeds aware of the notion that research transparency has been named the 'cornerstone of [this] methodological revolution',[115] where the open discussion of research development has been identified as the foundation of social science.[116] In this, the empirical portions of the interview data should not be confused with the core methodology that was used to generate the responsive-legality ideal type (although, in truth, the empirical material interacted iteratively with the literature review and analytical project to reveal this ideal type). Rather, the methodology pursued in generating the empirical material is discussed to reveal the ways that this material was itself scrutinised for the purposes of illustrating the features of the type analytically discerned (though not yet consciously distilled) prior to the treatment of the data.

Interviews

As has already been outlined,[117] the empirical research findings derive from forty semi-structured interviews with former RRT members; 10 of these composed two initial pilot studies, and 30 composed a later main study.

The former members had worked on the tribunal over a number of years – from as early as 1999 to as late as 2013 – and the interviewed participants roughly reflected the demographics of tribunal members over this period. All phases of the research obtained ethics approval from the Human Research Ethics Advisory Panel (HREA Panel B) at the University of New South Wales, and interviewees were recruited with the knowledge that their participation would be voluntary and anonymous.

When presenting the interview data, careful attention was also paid to preserving the anonymity of participants, given that participants had agreed to participate in the study on this basis. As such, participants' real names were replaced with pseudonyms and the gender of the participants was sometimes changed. Background reflections and personal anecdotes provided by the participants were discussed where they were deemed helpful for illustrating a richer picture of the broader issues raised in those interview portions, but careful attention was paid to remove anecdotes and information provided by participants that would allow them to be identified. At times this was difficult because some prominent members of the Australian legal, political and academic community were involved, and in these instances the information was presented in a necessarily vague manner. The background details of participants' lives are only preserved in the descriptions and analysis to the extent that they do not disclose the participants' identities: where particular biographical details appear somewhat unique, such as where the participant has written textbooks on refugee law, for example, this information is only shared where there are other potential individuals for whom this is the case.

The study's reliance on semi-structured or unstructured interviews is in keeping with other socio-legal studies that adopt this method because of its ability to reveal information that may not be provided through the narrower fully structured interview format or even more structured methods, such as surveys.[118] It might be likened to Laura Beth Nielson's approach in her study of the relationship between individuals' experiences with offensive public speech and their legal consciousness, for example.[119] Nielson asked individuals about their experiences with and understandings of racist speech, sexually suggestive speech and begging in public areas, allowing respondents to discuss and define for themselves what they considered to be offensive or problematic.[120] As the present study does,[121] she follows in the footsteps of Patricia Ewick and Susan Silbey, whose earlier work sought to provide a critical overview of legal consciousness typologies resulting from 141 interviews,[122] in which they asked respondents general questions about their everyday lives and the problems that they faced in their schools, workplaces and communities, allowing them to elaborate whether and in what ways they perceived the law to be important in these spaces.[123] The present study also pursues this approach in that the organic retrieval of information was facilitated through the semi-structured interview format.

The pilot interviews

Two pilot studies were conducted before the main study interviews took place. The first pilot study involved six refugee lawyers and academics specialising in refugee law participating in a 30- to 60-minute interview.[124] These initial pilot interviews combined open- and closed-ended questions, ultimately following a relatively rigid series of questions (compared to the main study, at least). At this early stage of the research, the research questions were loose and unconsolidated, yet, perhaps conversely, they were presented in an artificially narrow manner such that significant modifications were made between the pilot study and the main study approaches. At the point of conducting the pilot interviews, the substantive research questions were framed somewhat differently to those later presented in the main study. The pilot interviews all began in the same manner, with the participants being presented with a framework of factors that prohibit compliance with administrative law in judicial review.[125] Participants were asked to comment on the relevance of these factors to prohibiting compliance with administrative law in the RRT context. This framework spoke to the initial research question: in the early phases of the research, the enquiry was focused on the more narrow aspect of participants' legal knowledge. It was only after the pilot interviews had been conducted that the research question began to expand, as it became clear that the legal knowledge of the officials was itself embroiled in a range of broad and shifting normative and legal logics.

Participants, during the pilot interviews, were presented with Simon Halliday's framework of hypothesised factors influencing compliance with administrative law, which posits that compliance with administrative principles in judicial review is potentially constrained by three factors: the decision makers, the decision-making environment and the law.[126] It was explained to participants that the decision-making component was composed of the sub-categories of legal knowledge, legal consciousness and legal competence and that these three factors each influenced the extent to which the decision makers were able to comply with administrative law.[127] It was also put to participants that the present study was drilling deeper into what constitutes 'legal knowledge', adding greater detail and empirical validity to the original heuristic first developed by Halliday through interview and participant observation with front-line bureaucrats in Homeless Persons Units in the United Kingdom.[128] It was proposed to participants in the pilot study here that such knowledge may be influenced by a variety of factors, including, but not limited to, policy guidelines, professional networks, hierarchical structures, performance pressures and internal training. The hope was to elicit the participants' attitudes towards this newly devised framework of factors potentially influencing the officials' legal knowledge. These factors were also presented to participants in visual heuristic form to bring the participants' awareness back to considerations of these factors during the interview conversations.

The first pilot study revealed that the author was talking to the wrong people. Whilst knowledgeable about refugee law and refugee issues and often having had much experience with RRT practice and procedure (having, in the case of some interviewees, represented applicants in the RRT, attended meetings with RRT members, written academic papers about the RRT, produced Country Information reports used by RRT members or had other experience on boards and committees with RRT members), the advocates, lawyers and academics that the researcher spoke to were still not in a position to assess the legal knowledge of the decision makers. They could not get inside their heads and express their views in a way that was clearly and reliably digestible to the researcher, despite efforts sometimes to do so. This reality remained the case both for the subsequent re-articulation of the research question (pursuing the legal consciousness enquiry) and the final iteration of the research question – refined to explicitly consider the officials' normative administrative justice orientations that broadly *and* intimately enveloped their decision making.

The second pilot study therefore recruited former members of the RRT to attempt to assess the officials' legal knowledge by speaking to the officials themselves.[129] The same framework constructed by Halliday was presented to participants. It was proposed that their legal knowledge was influenced by a variety of factors, including policy guidelines, professional networks, hierarchical structures, performance pressures and internal training. However, the interviewees were often reluctant to talk about the framework posited. They viewed the proposed framework of factors influencing the decision maker's legal knowledge as simple, artificial, irrelevant or a combination of all three. They often acknowledged that legal knowledge in the tribunal was influenced by these factors, but they could not say to what extent this was the case and rather than providing concrete anecdotes that might illustrate the impact of these various factors on legal knowledge in the tribunal, they had bigger, broader questions of law, justice and morality in mind.

These interviews prompted revision of the core theoretical frame; in particular, they prompted abandonment of the quest to add further detail to Halliday's heuristic in search of understanding the more pervasive questions that burdened these contemporary officials in their daily decision making –shifting the analysis, first, onto the legal consciousness of the decision makers and, finally, more broadly still, to the normative logics that influence their conceptions of administrative justice. Such broadening out of the research question is similar to Ewick and Silbey's research modification in *The Common Place of Law*.[130] Ewick and Silbey initially set out to identify the number and kinds of potential legal problems that people experienced, to identify what people did about these situations and to see if there were differences by race in either the number or the kinds of problems that people experienced in their use of legal services.[131] As participants began to reveal broader attitudes towards law and its importance in their reflections, the study evolved from an initial range of narrow questions to 'other questions about the meaning and role of law in the lives of its citizens'.[132] Ewick and Silbey became more interested in wider accounts of legal consciousness as it became clear that participants' contributions did not provide concrete responses to their initially narrow questions, but instead opened up avenues to consider deeper questions of human consciousness that structure different images of legality.[133] They note,

> We did not begin the project with the theory fully elaborated in its current form. It developed out of an iterative process of data analysis and critical reflection about what we were finding in our respondents' comments. Thus the models of legality and legal consciousness that we developed were produced both deductively and inductively, working with existing theoretical and empirical literature and data we collected.[134]

The pilot interviews in this study inspired a similar combination of inductive and deductive processes, as well as the substantive shift towards considerations of legal consciousness and, in its final form, significant administrative justice changes echoed in a broad interdisciplinary public administration literature. Rather than providing information regarding the manner in which the factors proposed influence legal knowledge, many of the interviewees rejected the notion that legal knowledge was even a virtue that mattered in the first place. In place of discussing the importance of legal knowledge, participants discussed, for example, the role that personal experience played in shaping good RRT decision making and the way that truth verification was an important life skill for any administrative decision maker to make a just and fair decision.[135] Such discussions unearthed broader questions of the decision makers' normative values, shifting the enquiry to a consideration of the administrative justice frameworks motivating contemporary administration.[136]

The main study interviews

The main study drew on these pilot findings, modifying the initial approach taken in the pilot study in both substance and form. Rather than focusing on the factors that influence the officials' legal knowledge, the main study began to question the officials' broader attitudes towards law and justice. Whilst this was still different from the final iteration of the research question, it generally reflected the overall shift towards the emphasis on officials' normative logics that characterised the final research project.

A number of modifications to the interview structure were made to ensure that the findings of the main study were more telling than those of the pilot. These modifications involved, first, shifting from a predominantly closed approach to a loosely semi-structured approach. As the pilot study at times revealed, the predominantly closed approach produced somewhat artificial responses in that the participants were often led unwillingly to provide responses to a narrow range of questions that they deemed irrelevant to their decision making. Second, the use of leading questions was abandoned. This allowed interviewees to reveal their truthful and organic attitudes towards law without the interference of the narrow and somewhat artificial suppositions of the interviewer guiding their responses.

With methodological accuracy in mind, the transcripts of three participants were discarded from consideration because of their unreliability. One participant consistently demonstrated a lack of trust with the interviewer, making comments such as 'I don't feel comfortable talking about that',[137] and another offered only a 10-minute interview, claiming that her RRT work was so long ago that much of it was not fresh in her mind. The last of these claimed by written correspondence that he was a former member of the RRT but, upon commencing the interview, said that this had been in a formal capacity only; he had never actually decided RRT cases as he elected only to decide migration matters with the MRT. Though this participant provided some interesting insights with regards to his migration work, the transcript was disregarded to ensure consistency among respondents.

Transcript analysis

Once the interviews had been recorded and transcribed, they were coded and analysed. This constituted the lengthiest part of the empirical research process.

In the first few iterations of the research question, the pilot study transcripts were coded with the assistance of NVivo software to generate themes for closer independent analysis. The NVivo software was first used to unearth any common terms and themes raised throughout the transcripts. In the phase of solely pursuing the legal consciousness framework, terms such as *law* and *legal* were entered into the search domain to draw attention to passages where these terms may reveal more about officials' attitudes towards law. This reduced the time that would otherwise have been spent manually trawling through lengthy transcripts. Attention to such passages revealed, for example, that the terms *callous*, *superficial*, *ignorant*, *difficult* and *analytical* were all common terms accompanying the discussion of law, and these became the terms drawn on to reflect the findings at that stage of the research design.

However, the realisation after using this software to code various iterations of the research question was that it would ultimately not assist in producing meaningful data or rich conceptual and theoretical findings. This is demonstrated with regards to the way that the programme was utilised when pursuing the bureaucratic legal consciousness and administrative justice enquiry, discussed briefly here to illustrate.

In this stage of the research process, there was no way for the programme to qualify the nature of the relationship between these concepts and the legal consciousness of the participants. The number of times the word *experience* was used in close proximity to the word *law*, for example, would not reveal whether a valuation of experience resulted in a valuation or devaluation of law. Furthermore, whether the exact words thrown up the greatest number of times in the search were accurate reflections of the broader moral value that the participants were espousing was also something that would need further qualification through a detailed reading of the substantive content of the passages. For example, a close reading of the passages that utilised the word *knowledge* revealed that in these utterances participants were not necessarily discussing a value that was separate from *experience*. Closer reading revealed that 'experience' and 'knowledge' were actually concepts that the participants discussed in tandem; *knowledge* often referred to experiential or intuitive understandings of a country or place that were factually relevant to discerning the claim. Both *experience* and *knowledge*, when conceptualised this way, were actually common values that participants expressed when expressing 'against the law'[138] images of legality and could be understood under the umbrella conceptualisation of experience valuation. On the other hand, a term that was not utilised as commonly as the term *knowledge* – that is, the term *intellect* – was actually the *concept* that participants commonly expressed in contradistinction to 'experience' when expressing 'before the law'[139] images of legality.[140] It was nuances such as this that made an independent recoding of the themes unearthed, following the NVivo analysis, paramount.

Again, NVivo provided only limited guidance with regards to the narrower allocation of the interview material according to Ewick and Silbey's categories of law as 'handy', 'callous', 'superficial', 'culturally ignorant', 'constraining', 'irrelevant', 'lazy', 'frightening', 'difficult', 'reasoned', 'analytical', 'a map' and 'a shield'. The first step in allocating according to these divisions was to input into NVivo each of Ewick and Silbey's sub-categories, including, for 'before the law' 'constraint', 'capacity' and 'time and space'; for 'with the law' 'law as an instrument versus law as a game', 'law as a commodity', 'law as constraint', 'law as collective action' and 'law in time and space; and for 'against the law' 'arbitrariness', 'avoidance and resignation', 'constraint' and 'masquerade'. Again, it was clear that many of these terms did not assist in understanding the way that the participants truly thought about the law and its role in administering justice. Whilst the term *time*, for example, returned 204 hits, these hits were most commonly statements regarding the participant's 'time' on the tribunal, the interviewer thanking the participant for their 'time' or discussions regarding the 'time' taken to make a decision, for example. They showed no conceptual relationships that would assist in illustrating the actual values and justice orientations driving administrative action.

As such, by the time the final research question had been reached – in iteration and reiteration with the broad public administration literature – NVivo was not consulted to analyse the interview transcripts. Indeed, the final form of this book did not set out to prescriptively confine its framing to any particular semantic terms; it was more interested in identifying the deeper conceptual patterns that marked the officials' normative justice leanings. In this, the repeated scrutiny of interview material was able to capture and meaningfully illustrate the trends explored across a broad public administration literature, together demonstrating the emergent features of responsive legality explored in the subsequent chapters.

Notes

1 See, for example, Chris Grey and Christina Garsten, *Trust, Control and Post-Bureaucracy* (Sage Publications, 2001); Harro Hopfl, 'Bureaucratic Accountability in Britain: Some Sceptical Reflections' in Stewart Clegg, Martin Harris and Harro Hopfl (eds), *Managing Modernity: Beyond Bureaucracy* (Oxford University Press, 2011); Mats Alvesson and Stanley Deetz, 'Critical Theory and Postmodern Approaches to Organisational Studies' in Stewart Clegg, Cynthia Hardy et al (eds), *The Sage Handbook of Organisation Studies* (Sage Publications, 2006) 256.
2 Grey and Garsten, above n 1.
3 Hopfl, above n 1.
4 Jannis Kallinikos, 'Bureaucracy under Siege: On Information, Collaboration and Networks' in Stewart Clegg, Martin Harris and Harro Hopfl (eds), *Managing Modernity: Beyond Bureaucracy* (Oxford University Press, 2011).
5 Stephen Ackroyd, 'Post-Bureaucratic Manufacturing? The Post-War Organisation of Large British Firms' in Stewart Clegg, Martin Harris and Harro Hopfl (eds), *Managing Modernity: Beyond Bureaucracy* (Oxford University Press, 2011) 198.
6 Ibid.
7 Alvesson and Deetz, above n 1.
8 Refer to pages 7–8 in this book.
9 Paul Hoggett, 'New Modes of Control in the Pubic Service' (1996) 74 *Public Administration* 636.
10 Charles Heckscher, 'Defining the Post Bureaucratic Type' in Charles Heckscher and Anne Donnellon (eds), *The Post Bureaucratic Organisation* (Sage Publications, 1994) 15.

11 Ibid 15.
12 Paul Du Gay, 'Without Regard to Persons: Problems of Involvement and Attachment' in Stewart Clegg, Martin Harris and Harro Hopfl (eds), *Managing Modernity: Beyond Bureaucracy* (Oxford University Press, 2011).
13 Stewart Clegg, 'Under Reconstruction: Modern Bureaucracies' in Stewart Clegg, Martin Harris and Harro Hopfl (eds), *Managing Modernity: Beyond Bureaucracy* (Oxford University Press, 2011) 202–29.
14 Ibid.
15 B Guy Peters and Vincent Wright, 'Public Policy and Administration, Old and New' in Robert E Goodin and Hans-Dieter Klingemann (eds), *A New Handbook of Political Science in the Foundations of Bureaucracy in Economic and Social Thought* (Oxford University Press, 1996).
16 Ibid 628.
17 Ibid.
18 Refer to Chapter 1 of this book, pages 13 and 18.
19 Max Weber, *Economy and Society* (Roth & Wittich, eds, 1968).
20 Ibid 635.
21 Ibid.
22 Sharon Bolton, *Emotion Management in the Workplace* (Palgrave Macmillan, 2004) 13.
23 Ibid 14.
24 For further sources exploring the continued relevance of Weber's work to contemporary understandings of bureaucratic rationality and public organisations, see Harold Berman, 'Some False Premises of Max Weber's Sociology of Law' (1987) 65 *Washington University Law Quarterly* 758–70; Ferdinand Kolegar, 'The Concept of "Rationalization:" and Cultural Pessimism in Max Weber's Sociology' (1964) 5 *Sociological Quarterly* 355–73; Donald Levine, 'Rationality and Freedom: Weber and Beyond' (1981) 51(1) *Sociological Inquiry* 5–25; Joyce S Sterling and Wilbert E Moore, 'Weber's Analysis of Legal Rationalisation: A Critique and Constructive Modification' (1987) 2(1) *Sociological Forum* 67–89; Susan S Fainstein and Norman I Fainstein, 'The Political Economy of American Bureaucracy' in Frank Fisher and Carmen Sirianni (eds), *Critical Studies in Organisations and Bureaucracy* (Temple University Press, 1984) 311; Reinhard Bendix, *Max Weber: An Intellectual Portrait* (University of California Press, 1977); Jane Bennett, *The Enchantment of Modern Life: Attachments, Crossings, and Ethics* (Princeton University Press, 2001); Cary Boucock, *In the Grip of Freedom: Law and Modernity in Max Weber* (University of Toronto Press, 2000); Sally Ewing, 'Formal Justice and the Spirit of Capitalism: Max Weber's Sociology of Law' (1987) 21 *Law and Society Review* 488–513; Stephen Feldman, 'An Interpretation of Max Weber's Theory of Law: Metaphysics, Economics and the Iron Cage of Constitutional Law' (1991) 16 *Law and Social Inquiry* 205–48; William Hennis, 'Max Weber's "Central Question"' (1983) 12 *Economy and Society* 135–80; Stephen Kalberg, 'Max Weber's Types of Rationality: Cornerstones for the Analysis of Rationalization Processes in History' (1980) 85 *American Journal of Sociology* 1145–79; Anthony Kronman, *Max Weber* (Edward Arnold, 1983); Scott Lash and Sam Whimster, *Max Weber, Rationality and Modernity* (Allen & Unwin, 1987); Karl Löwith, *Max Weber and Karl Marx* (H Fantal ed, Allen & Unwin, 1982); Dragan Milovanovic, *Weberian and Marxist Analysis of Law* (Cambridge University Press, 1989); Wolfgang Schluchter, *The Rise of Western Rationalism: Max Weber's Developmental History* (University of California Press, 1981); David M Trubek, 'Max Weber on Law and the Rise of Capitalism' (1972) *Wisconsin Law Review* 720–53.
25 Bolton, above n 22, 18.
26 Ibid 19.

27 Steven Maynard-Moody and Michael Musheno, *Cops, Teachers, Counselors: Stories from the Front Lines of Public Service* (University of Michigan Press, 2003).
28 Ibid 3.
29 See this chapter, pages 44–50, for a detailed discussion.
30 *Tribunal Amalgamation Act 2015* (Cth).
31 Australian Government Administrative Appeals Tribunal, *Amalgamation of Tribunals* (22 September 2015) <www.mrt-rrt.gov.au/Amalgamation.aspx>.
32 Australian Government Administrative Appeals Tribunal, *Overview of Tribunals Scene Australia* (22 September 2015) <www.aat.gov.au/about-the-aat/engagement/speeches-and-papers/the-honourable-justice-garry-downes-am-former-pre/overview-of-tribunals-scene-australia>.
33 Australian Government Migration Review Tribunal – Refugee Review Tribunal, *Refugee Review Tribunal: An Overview* (21 September 2015) <www.mrt-rrt.gov.au/Files/HTML/R8-RefugeeReviewTribunalOverview-1012.html>.
34 Hereafter *Migration Act*.
35 Hereafter *Migration Regulations*.
36 Opened for signature 28 July 1951, 189 UNTS 151 (entered into force 22 April 1954) (hereafter '*Refugee Convention*').
37 Ibid art 1A.
38 See this chapter, pages 37–40, for further discussion of these guidelines.
39 *Migration Act* s 415.
40 Australian Government Migration Review Tribunal – Refugee Review Tribunal, *Our Role and Services* (21 September 2015) <www.mrt-rrt.gov.au/Applying-for-a-review/What-is-a-merits-review.aspx>.
41 As discussed by many former members in interview.
42 *Migration Act* s 424.
43 Section 424 does not apply where there has been an error of law which causes it to identify a wrong question, to ignore relevant material, to rely on irrelevant material or, in some circumstances, to make an erroneous finding or reach a mistaken conclusion affecting the tribunals exercise or purported exercise of power, thereby exceeding its authority or power: *Craig v South Australia* (1995) 184 CLR 163.
44 *Migration Act* s 417.
45 The Constitution of Australia.
46 Peter Cane, *Administrative Tribunals and Adjudication* (Hart Publishing, 2010) 3–6.
47 Ibid.
48 Ibid 197.
49 Refugee Convention art 1A.
50 Migration Act s 91R.
51 Migration Act s 36(2)(aa).
52 Interview with [Anonymous Participant M], (semi-structured interview) (17 December 2013); Interview with [Anonymous Participant Q], (semi-structured interview) (20 December 2013); Interview with [Anonymous Participant Y], (semi-structured interview) (28 January 2014).
53 Cane, above n 46, 4.
54 Drake v Minister for Immigration and Ethnic Affairs (1979) 24 ALR 577. See also Better Decisions: Review of Commonwealth Merits Review Tribunals, ARC Report No 39 (Canberra, Australian Government Publishing Service, 1995) viii.
55 Re Brian Lawlor Automotive vCollector of Customs (1978) 1 ALD 167, 177.
56 Commonwealth, Administrative Review Committee, Parliamentary Paper No 144 (1971) 5.

57 Cane, above n 46, 146. Cane notes that this is also a point made extra-judicially as early as 1980 by Brennan J. See F G Brennan, 'Comment: The Anatomy of an Administrative Decision' (1980) 9(1) *The Sydney Law Review* 2.
58 Kerr Committee Report, 62, in Cane, above n 46, 146.
59 Cane, above n 46, 162.
60 Ibid 163. Here Cane notes that deciding whether a decision under review is illegal or not is part of the function of merits review tribunals: Collector of Customs (NSW) v Brian Lawler Automotive Pty Ltd (1979) 2 ALD 1, 7 (per Bowen CJ).
61 Cane, above n 46, 163. Note that this is not a feature of the RRT's jurisdiction, but the discussion has been included here to outline the comparative differences between Australian tribunals and UK and US tribunals for a more international readership.
62 Leslie Zines, *The High Court and the Constitution* (The Federation Press, 5th ed, 2008).
63 Cane, above n 46, 164. On the distinction between void and voidable decisions, see Mark Aronson, Bruce Dyer and Matthew Groves, *Judicial Review of Administrative Action* (Lawbook Co, 5th ed, 2013).
64 Peter Cane, 'Merits Review and Judicial Review: The AAT as a Trojan Horse' (2000) 28 *Federal Law Review* 213.
65 Migration Act s 353 and 420.
66 Australian Government Migration Review Tribunal – Refugee Review Tribunal, Annual Report 2013–2014 <www.mrt-rrt.gov.au/AnnualReports/MRTRRTAR201314.pdf>.
67 Australian Government Migration Review Tribunal – Refugee Review Tribunal, Strategic Plan 2013–2016 <www.mrt-rrt.gov.au/About-Us/Our-role-and-services.aspx> 3.
68 Australian Government Migration Review Tribunal – Refugee Review Tribunal, Our Service Charter <www.mrt-rrt.gov.au/Conduct-of-reviews/Service-charter.aspx> (accessed 13 January 2015). The additional expectations that the tribunal says it will meet include that it will 'acknowledge applications for review in writing within two working days; include a contact name and telephone number on all our correspondence; help you to understand our procedures; provide information about where you can get advice and assistance; provide information so that you can engage effectively in the review process; provide you with advance notice of the time and place of hearing, if we invite you to a hearing; attempt to assist you if you have any difficulty understanding or participating in the review process; provide you with advance notice of the time and place of the hearing, if we invite you to a hearing; attempt to assist you if you have difficulty understanding or participating in the review process due to an age or physical, mental, psychological or intellectual condition, disability or frailty or for social or cultural reasons; provide reasons for our decisions; publish guidelines relating to the priority we give to particular cases; publish time standards within which we aim to complete reviews; abide by the Member Code of Conduct and publish information on caseload and tribunal performance'.
69 Australian Government Migration Review Tribunal – Refugee Review Tribunal, Annual Report 2013–2014, above n 67, vii. Note also that these Charters may make us think of Adler's consumer type, which draws part of its empirical inspiration from the use of Service Charters in the UK. The relevance of this to the core model presented in this book and suggestions for future research flowing from it are discussed further in Chapter 8.
70 Australian Government, Amalgamation of Tribunals <www.mrt-rrt.gov.au/Amalgamation.aspx>.
71 Cane, above n 46.

72 Migration Act s 474(1)(a).
73 Migration Act s 474(1)(b).
74 Migration Act s 474(1)(c).
75 Plaintiff S157/2002 v Commonwealth (2003) 211 CLR 476.
76 See SDAV v Minister for Immigration and Multicultural and Indigenous Affairs (2003) 199 ALR 43.
77 Craig v South Australia, above n 43, 14.
78 Ibid.
79 S A MaccDonald, *Judicial Review of Migration Decisions: How to Identify Jurisdictional Error in Asylum Cases* (Hansard Chambers, 2013) 10. Note, however, that this excludes errors regarding the content of foreign or international law (except to the extent that the relevant principles of international law are incorporated into domestic Australian law) because questions of foreign law or international law are considered to be questions of fact: Singh v Minister for Immigration and Multicultural Affairs (No 2) (2001) FCA 327 [22] (per Heerey J).
80 Australian Government Migration Review Tribunal – Refugee Review Tribunal, Employment Opportunities <www.mrt-rrt.gov.au/About-Us/Employment-opportunities.aspx> (accessed 4 January 2015).
81 As at the time of writing this section – 12 December 2014.
82 Migration Act s 397 and 460.
83 Migration Act s 353A and 420.
84 Migration Act s 407 and 472.
85 Australian Government Migration Review Tribunal – Refugee Review Tribunal, above n 86, 56.
86 Australian Government Migration Review Tribunal – Refugee Review Tribunal, Employment Opportunities <www.mrt-rrt.gov.au/About-Us/Employment-opportunities.aspx> (accessed 10 February 2016).
87 Data collated from biographical information available in Annual Report: Australian Government Migration Review Tribunal – Refugee Review Tribunal, Annual Report 07–08 <www.google.com.au/?gfe_rd=cr&ei=IA_HVJuiJrHu8wfNiYLIBQ&gws_rd=ssl#q=Annual+Report:+Australian+Government%2C+Migration+Review+Tribunal+%E2%80%93+Refugee+Review+Tribunal+Annual+Report+07-08>.
88 Being 17 of the 30 main study interviews.
89 Further detail is left deliberately vague to preserve the anonymity of former members.
90 Again, this detail is left deliberately vague to preserve the anonymity of former members.
91 As at the time of writing this section – 16 December 2014.
92 Australian Government, Migration Review Tribunal – Refugee Review Tribunal, above n 86, 133.
93 Interview with [Anonymous Pilot Participant 6], (semi-structured interview) (10 December 2013).
94 Australian Government, AUSTRAC Enterprise Agreement 2012–2014 (May 2012) 1.
95 Ibid.
96 Australian Government Migration Review Tribunal – Refugee Review Tribunal, above n 86, 60.
97 See Chapters 4, 5, 6 and 7 where further aspects of the interviewed participants' demographics are explored.
98 See Herbert M Kritzer, 'Research is a Messy Business: An Archeology of the Craft of Socio-Legal Research' in Simon Halliday and Patrick Schmidt (eds), *Conducting Law and Society Research* (Cambridge University Press, 2009)

264–85 for a discussion of the centrality of 'messiness' to the socio-legal research process.

99 This is a reference to Halliday and Schmidt's discussion of the centrality of serendipity to the socio-legal research process: see Halliday and Schmidt, above n 109, 5–6.

100 Trish Luker, 'Decision-Making Conditioned by Radical Uncertainty: Credibility Assessment at the Australian Refugee Review Tribunal' (2013) 25(3) *International Journal of Refugee Law* 502–34.

101 Interview with [Anonymous Pilot Participant 4], (semi-structured interview) (27 June 2013): 'Look that's a really interesting . . . it's really really interesting the work that you're doing and kind of in a way will also be the next step in what might have been the development in my work. I didn't encounter anyone who had come from a commercial law background. However, it doesn't surprise me; I mean, it fascinates me that you have that kind of anecdote to report and it certainly was something that I was trying to get . . . I think that my questions were somewhat constrained . . . in the interview, I think that one of my questions was around whether they felt that there had been increasing pressure to adjudicate/come to decisions more quickly or more efficiently, that sort of thing. And certainly they all said that the workload has escalated and there are protocols in relation to client management. But it could be I think that all the interviewees that I had spoken to were part of those tribunal members that the tribunal had picked, so there is a lot of caution on their part I think about saying very much. I did have informal discussions with ex tribunal members who were I think prepared to be a bit more outspoken. But I didn't record them, I just took the approach of chatting to various people on the phone and I, so um I wonder, if of course when you interview people in the context where that whole perception of somebody is dictated by the body itself. . .'.

102 Halliday and Schmidt, above n 100, 5.

103 Max Weber, *Economy and Society* Vol III (Harvard University Press, 1978) 650–78.

104 Refer to this chapter, pages 37–40.

105 As discussed in many interview conversations.

106 Refer to this chapter, page 39.

107 Refer to this chapter, pages 37–38.

108 Refer to this chapter, pages 39–40.

109 Ibid.

110 Refer to this chapter, pages 34–40.

111 See, for example, Heckscher, above, where Heckscher outlines that contemporary bureaucracy has seen global shifts towards more mixed and multifaceted systems of organisation where, for example, everyone takes responsibility for the whole rather than for a particular job only.

112 Refer, for example, to pages 32–40 of this chapter.

113 Ibid.

114 This refers to the way in which qualitative research may at times appeal to a few telling examples of a phenomena without any attempt to analyse less clear or contradictory data. David Silverman, *Doing Qualitative Research* (Sage Publications, 2010) 276.

115 Ibid.

116 Ibid.

117 As discussed in Chapters 1, 3 and 5.

118 See, for example, Patricia Ewick and Susan Silbey, *The Common Place of Law* (The University of Chicago Press, 1998); Laura Beth Nielson, 'Situating Legal

Consciousness: Experiences and Attitudes of Ordinary Citizens about Law and Street Harassment' (2000) 34(4) *Law and Society Review* 1061.
119 Nielson, above n 122, 1061.
120 Ibid 1058.
121 See Chapter 8 for detailed use of this framework to explore the ways officials' orientations to legality are composed of their normative justice orientations.
122 Note that 430 interviews were conducted altogether, but only 141 of these were transcribed and analysed to produce the findings.
123 Ibid.
124 These six interviews were conducted between May 2013 and June 2013.
125 Simon Halliday, *Judicial Review and Compliance with Administrative Law* (Hart Publishing, 2004).
126 Ibid.
127 Ibid.
128 See Halliday, above n 129, 20–8, for a discussion of the Homeless Persons Units used as the fieldwork site.
129 These eight interviews were conducted in July 2013.
130 Ewick and Silbey, above n 122.
131 Ibid 252.
132 Ibid.
133 Ewick and Silbey, above n 122.
134 Ibid 255.
135 See Chapter 5 of this book generally for a detailed discussion. See also Zach Richards, 'Unearthing Bureaucratic Legal Consciousness: Government Officials' Legal Identification and Moral Ideals' (2015) 11(3) *International Journal of Law in Context* 1–27.
136 Ibid.
137 Interview with [Anonymous Participant U], (semi-structured interview) (16 January 2014).
138 See Chapter 8 of this book for a more detailed discussion of 'against the law' images of legality.
139 See Chapter 8 of this book for a more detailed discussion of 'before-the-law' images of legality.
140 For example, participants discussed the importance of 'using one's own brain', 'being clever' and using 'smart tricks of logic', all notions that fall within the umbrella phenomenon of intellect idealisation despite participants only occasionally using this precise term. See Chapter 5 for the substantive discussion.

Reference list

Articles/books/reports

Ackroyd, Stephen, 'Post-Bureaucratic Manufacturing? The Post-War Organisation of Large British Firms' in Stewart Clegg, Martin Harris and Harro Hopfl (eds), *Managing Modernity: Beyond Bureaucracy* (Oxford University Press, 2011) 198

Alvesson, Mats and Stanley Deetz, 'Critical Theory and Postmodern Approaches to Organisational Studies' in Stewart Clegg, Cynthia Hardy et al (eds), *The Sage Handbook of Organisation Studies* (Sage Publications, 2006) 256

Aronson, Mark, Bruce Dyer and Matthew Groves, *Judicial Review of Administrative Action* (Lawbook Co, 5th ed, 2013)

Australian Government, *AUSTRAC Enterprise Agreement 2012–2014* (May 2012) 1

Bendix, Reinhard, *Max Weber: An Intellectual Portrait* (University of California Press, 1977)

Bennett, Jane, *The Enchantment of Modern Life: Attachments, Crossings, and Ethics* (Princeton University Press, 2001)

Berman, Harold, 'Some False Premises of Max Weber's Sociology of Law' (1987) 65 *Washington University Law Quarterly* 758–70

Bolton, Sharon, *Emotion Management in the Workplace* (Palgrave Macmillan, 2004)

Boucock, Cary, *In the Grip of Freedom: Law and Modernity in Max Weber* (University of Toronto Press, 2000)

Brennan, F G, 'Comment: The Anatomy of an Administrative Decision' (1980) 9(1) *The Sydney Law Review* 2

Cane, Peter, *Administrative Tribunals and Adjudication* (Hart Publishing, 2010)

Cane, Peter, 'Merits Review and Judicial Review: The AAT as a Trojan Horse' (2000) 28 *Federal Law Review* 213

Clegg, Stewart, 'Under Reconstruction: Modern Bureaucracies' in Stewart Clegg, Martin Harris and Harro Hopfl (eds), *Managing Modernity: Beyond Bureaucracy* (Oxford University Press, 2011) 202–29

Commonwealth, *Administrative Review Committee*, Parliamentary Paper No 144 (1971) 5

Ewick, Patricia and Susan Silbey, *The Common Place of Law* (The University of Chicago Press, 1998)

Ewing, Sally, 'Formal Justice and the Spirit of Capitalism: Max Weber's Sociology of Law' (1987) 21 *Law and Society Review* 488–513

Fainstein, Susan S and Norman I Fainstein, 'The Political Economy of American Bureaucracy' in Frank Fisher and Carmen Sirianni (eds), *Critical Studies in Organisations and Bureaucracy* (Temple University Press, 1984) 311

Feldman, Stephen, 'An Interpretation of Max Weber's Theory of Law: Metaphysics, Economics and the Iron Cage of Constitutional Law' (1991) 16 *Law and Social Inquiry* 205–48

Grey, Chris and Christina Garsten, *Trust, Control and Post-Bureaucracy* (Sage Publications, 2001)

Halliday, Simon, *Judicial Review and Compliance with Administrative Law* (Hart Publishing, 2004)

Heckscher, Charles, 'Defining the Post Bureaucratic Type' in Charles Heckscher and Anne Donnellon (eds), *The Post Bureaucratic Organisation* (Sage Publications, 1994) 15

Hennis, William, 'Max Weber's "Central Question"' (1983) 12 *Economy and Society* 135–80

Hoggett, Paul, 'New Modes of Control in the Public Service' (1996) 74 *Public Administration* 636

Hopfl, Harro, 'Bureaucratic Accountability in Britain: Some Sceptical Reflections' in Stewart Clegg, Martin Harris and Harro Hopfl (eds), *Managing Modernity: Beyond Bureaucracy* (Oxford University Press, 2011)

Kalberg, Stephen, 'Max Weber's Types of Rationality: Cornerstones for the Analysis of Rationalization Processes in History' (1980) 85 *American Journal of Sociology* 1145–79

Kallinikos, Jannis, 'Bureaucracy under Siege: On Information, Collaboration and Networks' in Stewart Clegg, Martin Harris and Harro Hopfl (eds), *Managing Modernity: Beyond Bureaucracy* (Oxford University Press, 2011)

Kolegar, Ferdinand, 'The Concept of "Rationalization": And Cultural Pessimism in Max Weber's Sociology' (1964) 5 *Sociological Quarterly* 355–73

Kritzer, Herbert M, 'Research Is a Messy Business: An Archeology of the Craft of Socio-Legal Research' in Simon Halliday and Patrick Schmidt, *Conducting Law and Society Research* (Cambridge University Press, 2009) 264–85
Kronman, Anthony, *Max Weber* (Edward Arnold, 1983)
Lash, Scott and Sam Whimster (eds), *Max Weber, Rationality and Modernity* (Allen & Unwin, 1987)
Levine, Donald, 'Rationality and Freedom: Weber and Beyond' (1981) 51(1) *Sociological Inquiry* 5–25
Löwith, Karl, *Max Weber and Karl Marx* (H Fantal ed, Allen & Unwin, 1982)
Luker, Trish, 'Decision-Making Conditioned by Radical Uncertainty: Credibility Assessment at the Australian Refugee Review Tribunal' (2013) 25(3) *International Journal of Refugee Law* 502–34
MacDonald, S A, *Judicial Review of Migration Decisions: How to Identify Jurisdictional Error in Asylum Cases* (Hansard Chambers, 2013) 10
Maynard-Moody, Steven and Michael Musheno, *Cops, Teachers, Counselors: Stories from the Front Lines of Public Service* (University of Michigan Press, 2003)
Milovanovic, Dragan, *Weberian and Marxist Analysis of Law* (Cambridge University Press, 1989)
Nielson, Laura Beth, 'Situating Legal Consciousness: Experiences and Attitudes of Ordinary Citizens about Law and Street Harassment' (2000) 34(4) *Law and Society Review* 1061
Review of Commonwealth Merits Review Tribunals, ARC Report No 39 (Canberra, Australian Government Publishing Service, 1995) viii
Richards, Zach, 'Unearthing Bureaucratic Legal Consciousness: Government Officials' Legal Identification and Moral Ideals' (2015) 11(3) *International Journal of Law in Context* 1–27
Schluchter, Wolfgang, *The Rise of Western Rationalism: Max Weber's Developmental History* (University of California Press, 1981)
Silverman, David, *Doing Qualitative Research* (Sage Publications, 2010)
Sterling, Joyce and Wilbert E Moore, 'Weber's Analysis of Legal Rationalisation: A Critique and Constructive Modification' (1987) 2(1) *Sociological Forum* 67–89
Trubek, David M, 'Max Weber on Law and the Rise of Capitalism' (1972) *Wisconsin Law Review* 720–53
Weber, Max, *Economy and Society* Vol III (Harvard University Press, 1978)
Weber, Max, *Economy and Society* (Roth & Wittich, eds, 1968)
Zines, Leslie, *The High Court and the Constitution* (The Federation Press, 5th ed, 2008)

Cases

Collector of Customs v Brian Lawler Automotive Pty Ltd (1979) 2 ALD 1
Craig v South Australia (1995) 184 CLR 163
Drake v Minister for Immigration and Ethnic Affairs (1979) 24 ALR 577
Plaintiff S157/2002 v Commonwealth (2003) 211 CLR 476
Re Brian Lawlor Automotive vand Collector of Customs (1978) 1 ALD 167
SDAV v Minister for Immigration and Multicultural and Indigenous Affairs (2003) 199 ALR 43
Singh v Minister for Immigration and Multicultural Affairs (No 2) (2001) FCA 327

Legislation

The Constitution of *Australia*
Tribunal Amalgamation Act 2015
Migration Act 1958
Migration Regulations 1994
The Convention Relating to the Status of Refugees 1951

Websites

Australian Government Administrative Appeals Tribunal, *Amalgamation of Tribunals* (22 September 2015) <www.mrt-rrt.gov.au/Amalgamation.aspx>

Australian Government Administrative Appeals Tribunal, *Overview of Tribunals Scene Australia* (22 September 2015) <www.aat.gov.au/about-the-aat/engagement/speeches-and-papers/the-honourable-justice-garry-downes-am-former-pre/overview-of-tribunals-scene-australia>

Australian Government, *Amalgamation of Tribunals* <www.mrt-rrt.gov.au/Amalgamation.aspx>

Australian Government Migration Review Tribunal – Refugee Review Tribunal, *Annual Report 07–08* <www.google.com.au/?gfe_rd=cr&ei=IA_HVJuiJrHu8wfNiYLIBQ&gws_rd=ssl#q=Annual+Report:+Australian+Government%2C+Migration+Review+Tribunal+%E2%80%93+Refugee+Review+Tribunal+Annual+Report+07-08>

Australian Government Migration Review Tribunal – Refugee Review Tribunal, *Annual Report 2013–2014* <www.mrt-rrt.gov.au/AnnualReports/MRTRRTAR201314.pdf>

Australian Government Migration Review Tribunal – Refugee Review Tribunal, *Employment Opportunities* <www.mrt-rrt.gov.au/About-Us/Employment-opportunities.aspx>

Australian Government Migration Review Tribunal – Refugee Review Tribunal, *Our Role and Services* (21 September 2015) <www.mrt-rrt.gov.au/Applying-for-a-review/What-is-a-merits-review.aspx>

Australian Government Migration Review Tribunal – Refugee Review Tribunal, *Our Service Charter* <www.mrt-rrt.gov.au/Conduct-of-reviews/Service-charter.aspx>

Australian Government Migration Review Tribunal – Refugee Review Tribunal, *Principal Member Direction 04 – Efficient Conduct of RRT Reviews* (October 2014) <www.mrt-rrt.gov.au/CMSPages/GetFile.aspx?guid=2f83d0c6-ecf4-4d1b-8440-45265361cf7d>

Australian Government Migration Review Tribunal – Refugee Review Tribunal, *Refugee Review Tribunal: An Overview* (21 September 2015) <www.mrt-rrt.gov.au/Files/HTML/R8-RefugeeReviewTribunalOverview-1012.html>

Australian Government Migration Review Tribunal – Refugee Review Tribunal, *Strategic Plan 2013–2016* <www.mrt-rrt.gov.au/About-Us/Our-role-and-services.aspx>

Moravcsik, Andrew, American Political Science Association, *Transparency: The Revolution in Qualitative Research* (January 2014) <www.princeton.edu/~amoravcs/library/transparency.pdf>

Other

Interview with [Anonymous Participant M], (semi-structured interview) (17 December 2013)
Interview with [Anonymous Participant Q], (semi-structured interview) (20 December 2013)
Interview with [Anonymous Participant U], (semi-structured interview) (16 January 2014)
Interview with [Anonymous Participant Y], (semi-structured interview) (28 January 2014)
Interview with [Anonymous Pilot Participant 4], (semi-structured interview) (27 June 2013)
Interview with [Anonymous Pilot Participant 6], (semi-structured interview) (10 December 2013)

3 Legitimating value

Responsiveness

Introduction

The legitimating value of responsive legality is responsiveness. When justifying their decisions according to this type, public officials value responsiveness in that they cling to a generalisation of purpose that aims to distinguish what is truly necessary for each particular applicant, rather than what has come to be taken for granted in traditions and routines.[1] They deeply value flexibility and adaptability and aim to deal with situations on a case-by-case basis, drawing firm justification for their decision from the extent to which they were able to adaptively respond to the overall set of circumstances that presented themselves in that particular case. In this sense, decision makers operating within this mode are chameleon-like and respond with enthusiasm to changed circumstances in the purposive pursuit of good outcomes.

Whilst we might remember the general discussion of flexibility, adaptability and responsiveness in the broader public administration literature in Chapter 2, this chapter draws on more closely related socio-legal studies to demonstrate, more concretely, the centrality of responsiveness as a valuable normative logic motivating contemporary public officials in justifying their decisions.

Socio-legal empirical studies of administrative justice and the small sub-field of bureaucratic legal consciousness, which has closely studied government official's attitudes towards law and justice, alongside the well-known social-theoretical jurisprudence of Nonet and Selznick together guide us towards considering the important role that responsiveness plays as a core legitimating value in responsive legality. The first part of this chapter explores these studies in detail, considering how responsiveness has been identified in existing scholarship as a feature of administrative governance. The second part of this chapter empirically illuminates the centrality of responsiveness to the responsive-legality ideal type through reference to the RRT interviews.

Responsiveness in social-legal empirical studies of administrative justice

In one of only three existing studies[2] on bureaucratic legal consciousness, Hertogh has identified that responsiveness is a core value motivating government officials in their decision making.[3]

By way of background, Hertogh's study builds on the bureaucratic legal consciousness work of Davina Cooper – the first study in this small socio-legal subfield. Cooper's study explores the relationship between the legal consciousness of British local government officials and juridification in the 1980s and 1990s. She draws on semi-structured interviews with approximately 60 local government actors (including councillors, officers and street-level workers) in education and corporate policy making in four urban areas. As she explains in her study, juridification – the central concept she uses to examine the legal consciousness of the government officials studied – can refer to many things: an expansion of legislation, new and significant litigation and judicial dicta or the sudden prominence of particular legal norms. Whilst, on any of these views of juridification, it had commonly been thought that such processes grant law a more prominent role within society, Cooper contends that such arguments do not allow us to understand what precisely this role is or when it might fluctuate or be hidden. In other words, without understanding the officials' attitudes towards juridification, we cannot achieve a complete picture of how the law works; the structure of the legal system alone will not provide the complete picture, as individual understandings will alter public officials' reception and application of the law. Hence, it is Cooper's goal to explore the complex and contradictory nature of legal consciousness and the overdetermination of juridification depending on alterations in political ideology, affiliation and institutional role. In her interviews with local government actors, Cooper finds six different images of law: law as a colonising force, law as a game/facilitator, law as a resource, law as a discourse, law as an environmental nuisance and law as means for conflict resolution or social consensus. She finds, common across these varying images of law, that many of these municipal actors, including politicians and policy makers, shared the same images of law as those of the everyday working-class poor.

Whilst Cooper does not utilise the language of responsiveness, some of its core features that she identifies – namely its complexity and contextual differentiation – are core features of responsiveness that might be discerned in the ideal type of responsive legality.

Where Cooper loosely identifies these values that might be associated with responsiveness, Hertogh's later study of bureaucratic legal consciousness explicitly names responsiveness as a core value that influences government officials' broad attitudes to law and justice.

Building on Cooper's study, Hertogh develops four profiles to explain government officials' attitudes towards the justice system. His study of front-line officials in the Netherlands and how these officials understand the *Rechtsstaat* (rule of law) constructs a series of normative profiles, arguing that bureaucrats can be divided between differing levels of legal awareness: from the legalists (officials who are well aware of the law and also identify with the law), the loyalists (officials with little awareness of the law but strong support for it), the cynics (officials with high awareness of the law but correspondingly high scepticism for it) and the outsiders (officials with little knowledge of, and little support for, the law).

In the study, Hertogh examines the extent to which the participant officials correctly conceive of the *Rechtsstaat* as it is understood in legal doctrine according to the values of legality, equality, fundamental rights, the separation of powers and the right to an independent court. He selects as his fieldwork site the 'Indonesian quarter', a small and predominantly blue-collar neighbourhood in the town of Zwolle in the eastern region of the Netherlands, and bases his observations regarding the legal consciousness of front-line officials on empirical material gleaned from a six-month evaluation study of the Neighbourhood Intervention Team Zwolle (NITZ Team), as well as on material from local and national Dutch newspapers.

Hertogh turns first to the question of awareness, applying what he considers to be an American conception of legal consciousness – where legal doctrine is treated as an independent variable to test awareness of law – through consideration of the NITZ Team's understanding of the legal principles of legality and equality that constitute part of the doctrinal substance of the *Rechtsstaat*. He finds that, although the principle of legality under Dutch law requires that every administrative act that affects the rights and freedoms of an individual should have a statutory basis, this principle did not play an important role in the front-line officials' day-to-day decision making. Rather, most decisions of the NITZ Team were largely informal and were not based on any official rules or regulations. He finds that

> whereas the legal ideal of the *Rechtsstaat* puts great emphasis on the rule of law and not of men, the members of the NITZ Team and other local officials seem to have changed this principle into a rule of men and not of law.[4]

Overall, the study finds that '[t]he NITZ Team was not oriented towards fitting their individual decisions into a system of general rules, but towards individual citizens and their unique circumstances'.[5] These officials demonstrated a 'personalistic value orientation'[6] that was also reflected in their value towards equality. They were less inspired by the idea of 'general justice',[7] which focuses on official rules and general norms, and more focused on the idea of individual justice, emphasising the importance of individual solutions for specific problems.

Hertogh's officials' motivating values therefore do not fit within any of the existing socio-legal administrative justice models. They do not strictly align with Mashaw's identified legitimating goals of accuracy and efficiency, service and fairness[8] (whilst they may align *most closely* with the legitimating value of fairness, as Adler identifies, this value is problematically tautologous and begs the question of what is meant by fairness in the first place),[9] and they do not align with Adler's identified values of accuracy, public service and legality. Instead, Hertogh's officials responsively emphasise the importance of individual solutions for individual problems, suggesting the existence of a new legitimating value outside of those devised in the pre-existing administrative justice models.

This is not to say that Hertogh's officials fully capture the new type of responsive legality presented in this book. They do not. Their preference for responsiveness to the exclusion of legality means that they demonstrate only limited features of the type. However, it does suggest the existence of broader legitimating values that might be considered alongside related literature and the empirical findings to necessarily build a fuller picture of twenty-first-century administrative justice.

Another socio-legal empirical work that illuminates the core role that responsiveness at times plays in motivating administrative decision making is Chris Jewell's *Agents of the Welfare State*.[10] Jewell's empirical study based on case studies across the US, Germany and Sweden finds that there are variations in the capacity of decision makers to be responsive across these different jurisdictions but that the capacity for responsiveness is greater across Germany and Sweden than it is in the US. Jewell finds that responsiveness is a core motivating value for administrators in Germany and Sweden because discretion is embedded in and justified by an extensive regulatory framework that continues to grow through the incorporation of legal and political decisions that revolve around the humanitarian question of what constitutes 'basic need'.[11] As such, in these European jurisdictions, there was a formal capacity to be responsive, whereas in the US, caseworkers have little formal independent role to play in determining the needs of claimants because their task has been reduced to a technical determination of 'eligibility' for a standardisation grant, rather than a more complicated evaluation of the overall needs of the applicant.

There is an interesting institutional component to Jewell's study, where Jewell shows that the maintenance of responsiveness in European public services is institutionalised through distinct professional traditions, legal foundations and resource networks. In contrast, over the years, US welfare agents have exercised a very limited capacity to be responsive in that they have had very little technical ability to infuse their own values and perspectives into their decisions. German caseworkers have far greater amounts of decision-making authority than do US caseworkers to be able to consider the particular situations of claimants in making needs-based assessments. Whilst German caseworkers can grant special needs payments to recipients for a broad range of household items and other expenses not covered by the monthly grant and can also make individual exceptions to a range of rules when deemed appropriate, the same is not the case in the US context.

Furthermore, Jewell finds that Swedish caseworkers do not have adequate opportunity to utilise their legal discretion under their current work conditions because of dramatic increases in caseload size during the economic recession of the 1990s. Increased caseloads have drastically affected Swedish workers by significantly limiting their potential to provide services directly in their capacity as social workers. Thus, Swedish caseworkers fall short of their responsive potential because agencies lack the organisational resources to create manageable work conditions and to instil caseworkers with the knowledge and values to make individualised but consistent assessments.

Overall, the US presents striking examples of caseworkers with limited capacity to be responsive, where standardised grants, standardised activation obligations and system complexity created by a range of narrowly targeted programmes largely preclude individualised considerations. By contrast, in both European nations, caseworkers have a greater mandate of authority and a wider range of choices, giving them a much more substantial role in tailoring aid to particular claimants' needs and interests. In this, they are more likely to demonstrate the value of responsiveness as they show adaptive and flexible decision making where outcomes and procedures applied may show subtle variations on a case-by-case basis.

With regards to the operation of responsiveness in the responsive legality ideal type, Jewell's study is illuminating as it reveals the perhaps obvious but very important point that decision makers' capacity for responsiveness will shift depending on the institutional context and technicalities of the legal and administrative regime that the decision maker is operating within.

Importing Nonet and Selznick's notion of responsive law

Nonet and Selznick's exploration of responsive law as a stage of legal development also helps to delineate the contours of the responsive-legality ideal type.

Sceptical of an unwavering emphasis on procedural regularity, Nonet and Selznick say that formal legal justice is not enough as it 'tends to serve the status quo'.[12] They go on to argue that

> [l]egal correctness has its own costs . . . substantive justice is undone when there is too great a commitment to upholding the autonomy and integrity of law. Rigid adherence to precedent and mechanical application of rules hamper the capacity of the legal system either to take new interests and circumstances into account or to remedy the effects of social inequality.[13]

For Nonet and Selznick, formal justice corresponds closely with what they call 'autonomous law' as opposed to the 'responsive law' that they champion.[14] Though it has its advantages over repressive governance and is sometimes a required precursor to, or dimension of, responsive governance, they argue that the sort of justice secured by autonomous law – regular, procedural and formalistic – is far from the sort of justice we should cherish as the desired outcome of law; it is far from the highest form of justice to which a legal system should aspire:

> Substantive justice is a derivative, hoped for by product of impeccable method. But formal justice is consistent with serving existing patterns of privilege and power . . . The justice of autonomous law is experienced as sham and arbitrary when it frustrates the very expectations of fairness it has encouraged. In time, the tension between procedural and substantive justice generates forces that push the legal order beyond the limits of autonomous law.[15]

This movement away from pure procedural justice and formal law – the shift towards responsive law – is for Nonet and Selznick 'the true program of sociological and realist jurisprudence'.[16] Responsive law seeks to preserve the positive aspects of autonomous law and transcend its limitations. Whilst autonomous law protects formal legal entitlement and procedural fairness, responsive law additionally considers the circumstances of social need and substantive justice (which, as this book finds, is the equality orientation of responsive law and the focus of Chapter 4). Whilst autonomous law aims to strictly enforce general rules according to their settled legal application, responsive law is oriented towards the legal principles implicit in these rules and the public purposes that they are designed to advance. And where autonomous law faithfully preserves procedural routines in the interest of the legal order's institutional independence, responsive law is conscious of the need for flexibility, openness and the merging of powers among the varied institutions of law and governance in order to achieve collective welfare and social justice. Responsive law is 'higher' in the sense that it resolves the important problem of establishing political order, a condition from which the legal and political system can move on to 'higher' pursuits.

Whilst Nonet and Selznick emphasise the overall state of responsive law as a broader system, and the emphasis in this book is on the ideals and normative logics driving administrative action, the notion of responsiveness that underpins their vision of responsive law can be explored alongside the socio-legal administrative justice and public administration studies to reveal that there is indeed a higher form of administrative justice that decision makers sometimes use to justify their decisions. In the process of justifying their decisions according to the motivating value of responsiveness, decision makers are not singularly asserting rights through the straightforward application of the law, as Adler's legal type captures,[17] nor are they dismissive of the law, as Mashaw's moral judgement model suggests.[18] Rather, they move flexibly with the law – specifically considering the law's purpose, its contextual relevance in broader sociological realities and its adaptability to a range of real-world scenarios that require its subtle manipulation to achieve fair outcomes whilst its basic skeleton is preserved.

As Nonet and Selznick were aware, responsive law is not immune from criticism – and neither is the value of responsiveness that administrative decision makers are motivated by in justifying their decisions according to responsive legality. One critique that Nonet and Selznick levy against responsive law more broadly is that it may weaken the consistency of procedure and allow citizens to more easily do as they wish. The criticism is that the law then loses its capacity to properly restrain individuals and command obedience. On this view, unaccountable discretion is alien to legal ordering, both because it might enable 'nine old men' to enact their preferences into law and because legal institutions are made particularly vulnerable to pressures of the political environment.

However, responsive law suggests a capacity for responsible, and therefore discriminate and selective, adaptation. It sees social pressures as sources of knowledge and important opportunities for self-correction. In doing so, it rectifies the deficiencies in a formalist rule-bound institution, which is poorly equipped to recognise what is actually at stake in its conflicts with the surrounding social world. Repressive and autonomous law is likely to adapt opportunistically because it lacks the criteria for rational reconstruction; it is only when an institution is truly purposive, as is the case in responsive law, that there can be both integrity and openness, rule and discretion. Responsive law presumes that individual purpose can be made objective enough and authoritative enough to control adaptive rule-making. Likewise, it is this basic set of criteria that administrative officials cling to in normatively justifying their decisions on the basis of responsive legality – they demonstrate integrity and openness, rule application and discretionary decision making; constantly striving to balance this mix of criteria in the responsive pursuit of administrative justice.

One related crucial feature in the officials' application of responsiveness as the legitimating value of responsive legality is a subtle awareness of the generalisation of law's objectives. As Nonet and Selznick explain, the critical step in the overall transition from autonomous to responsive law is the generalisation of law's objectives where particular rules, policies and procedures begin to be regarded as instrumental and expendable. In responsive law (as in responsive legality) the emphasis shifts to general goals and there is a new search for the implicit values inherent in rules and policies. In this process, the generalisation of purpose is a core source of flexibility within the modern organisation. For example, this generalisation of purpose might be seen where a university takes a step forward towards responsiveness as it learns to distinguish what is most necessary for the pursuit of higher learning from what it has come to take for granted in its traditions and routines. Responsive law therefore builds on the limitations of autonomous law in that it looks for purpose in the elaboration of rules and recognises that if rules are to be applied with precision, events must be classified accurately. This is an important development from autonomous law because rules necessarily depend for their relevance and role on the viability of appropriate historical conditions; as circumstances change, rules must be refashioned both to protect the needs of policy and to protect the authority of the rules themselves.

Amidst this blend of strengths and shortcomings, the primary advantage of responsive law – or, in the context of administrative decision makers providing normative justifications for their decisions, responsive legality – is that, in its emphasis on principle, it is a rich resource for criticising the authority of specific rules. Under this model, whilst a rule might meet the official criteria for legal validity, it might also be helpfully reassessed in light of its consequences for the values that are at stake. As Nonet and Selznick outline, an emphasis on purpose and context helpfully enhances rationality in legal reasoning, though the increase of purposiveness in law means that it becomes increasingly difficult to distinguish legal analysis from policy analysis and legal rationality from other forms of systematic decision making. However, with this opportunity cost, purposive legal thought also reduces the tendency for officials to retreat behind specific rules and escape responsibility. For purpose to gain authority, law must be able to elaborate the mandates of legal institutions, such that a critical phase of responsive law is the definition of mission, or the transformation of general purpose into specific objectives. In this sense, purposiveness requires inquiry into substantive outcomes and the consideration of what is factually needed to effectively fulfil institutional responsibilities. Otherwise put, purposive law is result-oriented, significantly departing from an emphasis on procedural justice in autonomous law, which is ignorant of consequences.

In this responsive system, important acknowledgement is made of the fact that to determine the rights and wrongs of a particular case is to take into account multiple outcomes, constraints and practical alternatives. This is partially attributable to the wide variability of legal authority, which stems from many factors, including the explicitness and clarity of rules and opinions, the consistency of enforcement and the weakening of consent. Further influencing this variability is the fact that rules differ markedly in terms of how and to what extent they impose obligations, with some rules being facilitative rather than prescriptive, and their main sanction for non-compliance therefore being rule followers' failure to achieve their purposes. The last contributing factor to this variability is that legal casuistry generates elaborate techniques for calculating the situational authority of legal principles: the abstract or dogmatic authority of a rule never fully determines what force the rule may have in the circumstances of a particular case. Given this variability in legal rules, in recognising the complexity of legal judgement and relaxing the claim to obedience, responsive law – and, likewise, decision makers justifying their decisions according to responsive legality – points to a larger ideal: it brings a promise of civility to the way law is used to maintain and define public order. In this emphasis, respect is a core virtue of civility, and all who share in the social environment are granted a presumption of legitimacy. Purposive law creates a sense of civility because it is informed by an 'ethic of responsibility' rather than an 'ethic of ultimate ends'.[19] Within this ethic of responsibility one is concerned about the foreseeable accounts of one's actions and therefore may consider multiple interests and competing and complementary values. Most specifically, responsive law nurtures civility in two senses. First, it overcomes the closed-mindedness of communal morality. In this, the growing authority of purpose weakens both prescription and symbolism; instead, purposive law demands that custom is morally justified by a rational assessment of costs and benefits. The result is that the legal order becomes 'civilised' in the sense that it is more refined, is receptive to cultural diversity and is less prone to brutalise the outsider or the eccentric. In this responsiveness, law aims to clarify the values at stake in the moral order, therefore ridding the culture of its insular elements. Furthermore, responsive law encourages a problem-centred and socially integrative approach to public crises. Because it is more interested in outcomes, it is more ready to utilise political resources. Whilst in this sense it shares an affinity with repressive law, repressive law differs in that it is fundamentally uncivil and opposed to the group structure of society: it manipulates power in single-minded defence of domination. Where responsive law is marked by purposive and civil regard for multiple ends and interests, responsive law is responsibly negotiated rather than won through subordination.

In the end, responsive law and decisions justified according to responsive legality encourage a fuller realisation of individual justice over the long term. Whilst the 'master ideal' of responsive law is legality (and thus much more is needed to capture this normative state than Mashaw's moral judgement captures in its neglect of legality),[20] this should not be confused with the notion of 'legalisation':[21] the proliferation of rules and procedural formalities. Instead, the ideal of legality should be cured of formalism and perceived more broadly (and it is this broadening that captures something distinct from Adler's legal type, something broader than its component feature of 'asserting rights').[22] In a properly purposive system, legality is the progressive reduction of arbitrariness and the creation of a system of law that is capable of reaching beyond mere formal regularity and procedural fairness to produce substantive justice.[23] With this in mind, it is reiterated here that the same can be said of decision makers driven by values of responsiveness. Officials toiling responsively have lost faith in the ability of the law to produce *enough justice*, though this is not to say that they do not appreciate the role of legality in achieving a purposive and outcome-oriented governance. Relatedly, the key function of administrative leadership in this mode is the 'institutional embodiment of purpose'.[24] In this, responsive law 'is no maker of miracles in the realm of justice; rather, its achievements depend on the will and resources of the political community'.[25]

As such, the unifying features of responsive law and governance, argued here to be usefully applied to illuminate the diverse features of purposive outcome-driven rule application and bureaucratic prioritisations of substantive justice in motivating officials and organisations employing the normative logics of responsive legality, include a number of elements. In one respect, as outlined previously, responsive-legal development allows legal reasoning to be more purposive to achieve the goal behind the rule and not simply the rule itself. As a flow-on effect, this purpose makes rigid procedural conformity less strict, which, in turn, invites the possibility of broader values shaping the operationalisation of the legal order. As such, the legal order becomes increasingly open and flexible and legal advocacy takes on a heightened politicism, whereby political forces help improve and change legal institutions but simultaneously threaten to undermine institutional integrity. Again this means that the authority of legal purpose to bring about substantive justice for applicants depends on the design of more competent legal institutions.

Empirical reflections: responsiveness in the RRT

There were many moments when participant RRT officials appeared to be driven by values of responsiveness, similar to Hertogh's NITZ Team officials and as explored by Nonet and Selznick in relation to systems of responsive law more broadly. As the responsive-legality ideal type broadly posits, RRT officials normatively justifying their decisions in this mode were adaptive and flexible and demonstrated a unique concern for blends of substantive and procedural justice, continually reiterating the importance of applicant welfare. They were chameleon-like and flexible and argued that their decisions were most justified when they took the particular concerns of the refugee applicant into consideration, sensitively and perceptively working with the law to achieve a fair outcome. They were not acting out of an innate self-interest or desire for reappointment of tenure but were more focused on the needs of the applicant and the importance of making a lawful decision that prioritised the individual's unique needs.

When operating within this mode, participant officials reflected that outcomes cannot be known before the case is provided to them but must be open to interpretation and dependent on the particularities of each case before them.[26] They therefore expressed a level of comfort in responsively adapting the purposes of the law to suit applicant needs. Where Ewick and Silbey found that citizens often act strategically in relation to legal actors, organisations and rules, those RRT members interviewed in this study demonstrated a similar responsiveness in the sense that they interpreted the law strategically to achieve particular outcomes that they deemed desirable. A useful motif illustrating the legal attitudes and justice orientation of these citizens and officials alike is the image of law as a game. In this image, 'law makes available tools, resources, symbols, and vocabularies useful in the construction of social life'.[27]

This notion of law as a game was also explored in Sally Engle Merry's study of the legal consciousness of working-class Americans and their experiences with courts and mediation.[28] Merry found that with greater experience in court, citizen users of courtrooms gradually shift from viewing the courtroom as awesome and fear inducing to seeing it as a complex institution that can be used as an arena for manipulation and play, 'a place to toy with enemies and to gain strategic successes by pummelling one's opponents with legal charges and summonses, even if no serious penalties are forthcoming'.[29] She goes so far as to say that some come to regard the law as entertainment, 'as a place to try out dominance games with others and see what will happen'.[30] The RRT officials interviewed in this study commonly shared these citizens' images of law as a game, viewing the law as a handy tool that could be used to achieve the outcomes that one desired: often, as discussed here, the desire for fair outcomes for the applicant.

One proponent of this story of law as 'handy' – something to be responsively and adaptively employed to produce a good, procedurally correct and substantively just decision – was Daniel Rogers.[31] Rogers was a former academic and refugee advocate. He had been working as a researcher before beginning on the tribunal and approached his research from a human rights and refugee activist perspective. Like many RRT members, he had worked for a number of charities to assist in providing refugees support and housing. He fondly discussed his experiences counselling and supporting these individuals who were on various community release programmes and expressed a recurring bitterness towards mandatory detention, which he had worked with a number of solicitors, barristers, academics and politicians to fight against.

When asked specifically about an influential and well-known case, *Chan Yee Kin*,[32] and the effect that it had on his decision making, Rogers responded,

> Well, I suppose that you go back to your own expertise. Real chance, many cases being, was: 'here is the Country Information'. Here are these claims usually made in fairly dramatic and sometimes extreme terms. How do I read

> the Country Information/the circumstances that this person would go back to? Because that's really the bottom line. At the end of the day, are you going to send them back or not? And so the real chance test is really just a very handy cluster of considerations to me about 'if the applicant's sent back, is there a real chance of serious harm?' And that was a – I mean, you can think of it in terms of eccentric [presumably meaning concentric] circles, there is a context that you know that is pretty unsatisfactory in itself. If you've done 20 years of international relations, you've got a pretty good idea of what it is.

For Rogers, the law was not an impediment to good decision making; it was a tool to be used to provide a fair outcome for the applicant. It was something to work with, continually responding to the needs of the applicant through subtle adaptation and application. The purpose of the law was central to this mode of decision making, as Rogers reminds us that 'claims are usually made in fairly dramatic and sometimes extreme terms'. Expounding the virtues of responsive decision making, Rogers expresses the importance of considering the context in which the applicant makes their claim, and purposively applying the law in the caring pursuit of the individual's welfare.

For Rogers, the law provides a 'handy cluster of considerations' that reflect the common sense that an individual could also gain through personal experience. Both the legal principle and the personal experience of the decision maker were valuable tools for answering the central question regarding the applicant's welfare: 'Are you going to send them back or not?' Rogers saw no problem in using the law to achieve just outcomes for the applicant. Both the law and the personal experience of the decision maker could be mobilised to answer the important question regarding the applicant's welfare: 'If the applicant's sent back, is there a real chance of serious harm?'

Rogers offered that he was a 'true believer' in refugee rights, and – through his discussions of his experiences with refugee advocacy agencies and refugee-related research and activism – presented a vision of administrative justice that focused closely on a consideration of the applicant's welfare.

In this sense, Rogers's narrative of law as 'handy' was clearly driven by broader understandings of the social constituency of the law; it was a tool to achieve certain processes and purposes by the individuals who enacted it. Just as law was a 'game' for some of Ewick and Silbey's citizen participants, Rogers saw his role as an official like a player in a game. He was intent on winning a good outcome for the applicant where they were deserving.

Similarly displaying this perception of law as a 'handy' game to be played to ensure fair outcomes for applicants was Germaine Thompson.[33] Thompson was a barrister of nearly two decades. She had written a number of leading Australian legal textbooks in a range of legal areas, and – at a relatively young age – had already had a high-profile legal career. Her barrister's chambers were lined with wigs, gowns, textbooks and dusty Commonwealth Law Report collections. She sat at a large wooden table and discussed her years working on the tribunal as a recent law graduate, and the youngest member of a mature and experienced group of officials. Thompson was highly knowledgeable about the law, discussing in detail various legislative provisions and High Court cases. However, whilst these laws were central to Thompson's descriptive reflections –insofar as she recurrently discussed the various sections and tests that would guide her decision making – they were important only in that they provided a decision-making template and required little more than formal regurgitation to produce a favoured outcome in the written reasons.

Thompson discussed the way the courts in judicial review provided very little guidance for RRT decision making, and yet, the decision makers would need to work the law strategically into their decisions so that the courts would be satisfied with the outcome and the correct factual outcome could therefore be made. In this discussion, Thompson reflected that being unaware of the full range of facts presented by applicants meant that the courts were often ignorant of the intricate reasons that motivated the tribunal's decisions, sloppily applying a series of largely irrelevant rules to determine whether the allegedly correct decision had been made. She asserted that the Federal Court and the Federal Magistrates Court 'don't really know how the system works from the inside', and as a result that judges would sometimes assume that just because a person was represented by a lawyer in the tribunal, all the material that was discussed during the course of the hearing was relevant and therefore should not be overturned. For Thompson, this was a simple and erroneous generalisation, and the reality of the complex RRT decision making was that the facts were often so complicated and contentious that they would be handled poorly by the decision maker, and a poor decision would be set in stone because it would fall through the cracks of the courts on judicial review. As a result, law was merely a game to be played to achieve the proper outcome. It was subjectively constructed and applied, and therefore to be rightfully appropriated for the purposes of protecting the applicant through ensuring the delivery of a fair outcome that was conscious of the complex factual intricacies of the claim to which the courts were often oblivious.

For Thompson, this meant that

> once you got to the court you were so hamstrung and you had to make it look like you're not looking at the merits when really everyone knows that you are. And the courts try to make it seem like they're looking at it as a matter of legal error. This is nonsense, really.

The law was therefore something to be used by the decision maker 'for the greater good' and 'as part of the artificialities that we were all aware of'. As was the case for Rogers, the value underpinning Thompson's blend of moral and legal concerns to justify her decisions was clearly an adaptive responsiveness: a purpose-oriented application of the law that mutated according to the facts and needs of each unique applicant.

Frank Grey,[34] who had extensive foreign affairs experience before beginning on the tribunal, again epitomises this responsive drive that characterises decision making justified according to responsive legality.

Grey had not studied law, but he did not see this as an obstacle to good decision making. In fact, Grey was keen to emphasise that he was not a lawyer, nor did he desire to be one. He recounted that he told the head of staff when he began on the tribunal: 'I hope the department doesn't think that I'm a lawyer', to which the head of staff responded, '[T]he tribunal knows exactly what you are'. Grey was happy self-identifying instead as 'if anything, a historian and an economist'. For Grey, it was not important to identify as a lawyer because it was the purpose of the law that mattered when making a good decision, which he believed non-lawyers could equally decipher.

Grey had worked for a number of diplomatic agencies and United Nations branches across a range of African and South American countries and had spent much time with refugee applicants themselves in their home countries. Grey told detailed anecdotes of his experiences in Somalia, Uganda and Kenya, often reflecting on the differences between the reality of those individuals' lives and the ignorant view a Westerner might have of the daily struggles faced by African refugees.

When asked how the decision making of RRT officials could be improved, Grey responded,

> When I first joined the tribunal there were a lot of ex foreign affairs officers on the tribunal . . . They had a very good ability to analyse the situation in foreign countries. They understood third world countries; they'd lived in third world countries. I think there is a tendency now to increase the number of lawyers on the tribunal, and I think there are comparatively few ex foreign affairs officers or people with overseas experience. And I think decision making has deteriorated as a result. Which may not be what you want to hear . . . but I think it's a problem that . . . I think you really do need on a tribunal like the Refugee Review Tribunal for members to be multiskilled . . . You need to have a capacity for members to understand foreign countries, foreign cultures, and to really hear very carefully what the person is saying to you and to understand um their background. And if you've never lived outside Australia, it doesn't matter how smart you are . . . it's going to be more difficult for you.

For Grey, intelligence was not an important ingredient for good decision making, and neither were corresponding visions of rational administration. For Grey, 'it doesn't matter how smart you are'. Instead, good decision makers were multiskilled and had life experience in different countries and cultures that enabled them to truly understand the depth of issues faced by applicants. The law was a superficial body of rules that did not allow for deep understanding or analysis of the plight of the applicant, which was crucial for the production of good administration and the attainment of substantive justice. In this discussion, Grey was cynical of the belief that merely applying the law would be enough. He discussed that the law, on its own, was a superficial device often used to protect one's own decision from jurisdictional error but not enough in and of itself to achieve a fair outcome for the applicant. He posited,

> But um in terms of the law or misapplication of the law, normally that results in a wrong decision, because if there is a misapplication of the law by the tribunal then the Federal Magistrates Court – Federal Circuit Court, as its now called – will quickly send it back to the tribunal to be done again . . . but this means that the member who made the decision has just written it up wrong or to sum up a procedural error, and that's why it's remitted by courts. And the problem in my view is that the courts have no right to look behind the merits of a case as distinct from the legalities of the case; and if a person has been written up well by the member, it doesn't matter how bad the members' understanding of the country situation is, for example, the case will survive challenge in the court. And to me, that's a much more serious problem, and you see that in inconsistencies that there are within the tribunal between some members who will routinely remit departmental decisions, for example on Hazaras from Afghanistan, and other members who will routinely affirm those decisions, and that's very serious . . . and not enough attention, in my opinion, is paid to the inconsistencies between members. I mean I think it is right that members be allowed to make decisions freely and independently, and that's correct. But where you see a pattern of inconsistent approach to Country Information, I think much greater effort needs to be paid by the management of the tribunal to get members together and to try to reach some kind of common understanding about what's going on in the country concerned to minimise that. Because that results effectively in injustice to somebody when there's a clear misunderstanding of the country situation; and that's not a legal point, but it certainly is a very important point for the applicants.

For Grey, remitting a decision back to the tribunal was simply a reflection of the decision maker having followed the incorrect process, wrapped up under the pretence of an application of law. This, for Grey, was merely ancillary to the primary task of coming to a correct decision: a decision which is fair to the applicant. According to Grey, following the process of the law alone would not result in justice being done; it would only result in the appearance of justice. He went on to recount,

> I mean some of the errors I have to say can be pretty trivial. I had one of my decisions overturned in court for example because the letter . . . this was in the early days when the letter covering the invitation to a hearing was drafted by one of the staff. Now it's all computerised. But in those days it was drafted

> by one of the staff and the staff member um sent the letter correctly to the ahh applicant's agent but in the salutation at the beginning of the letter put 'Dear Miss agent' instead of 'Dear Mr. applicant', and so the Federal Magistrate said that the person had not received a valid application to a hearing and so everything that followed it . . . Even though no one noticed it until some clever clerk in the Federal Magistrates office noticed it . . . it was sent back to the tribunal to do again. Um. But so, you know, jurisdictional error comes in many shapes and sizes . . . that one I found a bit irritating.

Here, Grey recounted that something as superficial and unimportant as a letter being addressed to the wrong individual – even if it effectively reached the right person – could be seen as a procedural error in law and result in the decision needing to be made again. For Grey, this was 'laughable' and 'irritating' and a stark contrast to the important justice that could actually be done through the purposive interpretation and application of law for the factual discernment of the authenticity of the applicant's claim.

When asked specifically whether there was value in changing the tribunal from a single-member to a multi-member tribunal, Grey drew the conversation back to the consideration of the importance of personal experience and the centrality of personal experience to achieve corresponding visions of substantive justice for the applicant:

> You can't imagine how different it is living in a third world country to living in Australia. Even in a relatively advanced third world country. And to understand the culture of other countries – but to really understand, not just read a book or understand the legal reasons – but to know the people, to have talked to them, to have been in their homes and sort of know the way that they think and live and what it's like.

For Grey, good RRT decision making was defined by the decision maker's ability to truly understand the applicant – 'to know the people, to have talked to them, to have been in their homes and sort of know the way they think and live'. In these moments, the personal experience of the decision maker was idealised as the core mechanism for the overarching goal of reaching the correct outcome for the applicant. The law was not something to be rejected or overlooked; it was to be purposefully and selectively applied in the responsive pursuance of a substantively fair outcome.

To take one final example to demonstrate, Cate Arnolds displayed many of the features of responsiveness already explored in relation to Grey, Thompson and Rogers. Arnolds[35] had worked in a number of roles before beginning on the tribunal, including having worked in a legal capacity for government and in a number of human rights organisations. Her level of engagement in her decision making is reflected in her account of her first positive refugee assessment. She prided herself on her ability to empathise with the applicants and to get to the bottom of their stories to ascertain the genuineness of the claims that were presented. She gave the example of an applicant who had been a filmmaker in Iran who initially presented a somewhat confusing story in the hearing. The solution, arrived at through her experience working in human rights organisations with vulnerable applicants, was to tell the applicant to go away and to return to the hearing in a week's time when they were both thinking more clearly so that she could 'get everything straight'.

For Arnolds, it was incredibly important when conducting tribunal decision making to be able to empathise with people. She recounted, '[I]f you didn't have experience of some sort, I think you would struggle'. In these moments, the ability to achieve correct outcomes for applicants, as for her Iranian filmmaker, came primarily through the broader capacity to empathise and respond flexibly and responsively to a range of different circumstances.

Conclusion

This chapter has revealed the centrality of responsiveness as the core motivating value in the ideal type of responsive legality. Decision makers justifying their decision on this basis selectively adapt to changed circumstances by generalising the law's purpose to suit the needs of the applicant. This is not to say that they change the law or that they deviate from its structure and content. Rather, they perceive the viable margins of movement that the law may allow and sensitively seek to work within these margins in the pursuit of substantively fair outcomes.

Where Hertogh's NITZ Team officials were revealed to demonstrate the value of responsiveness, they did so to the detriment of rule-of-law compliance. Their rejection of legality in preference for responsiveness risks the decline towards repressive governance that Nonet and Selznick warn against. Something more than standalone responsiveness is therefore captured in the responsive-legality type: a responsiveness driven by sensitivity to the importance of procedural compliance.

Officials driven by responsiveness believe that the law is a tool that can be subjectively constructed with a range of purposes in mind, therefore inviting the pursuance of one's own justice-oriented purposes in applying it. In these moments, rigid conformity to law is not enough to produce justice in terms of ensuring fair *outcomes* for applicants. Where the law obviously cannot fully embody human experience or factual truthfulness, it is correspondingly perceived as limited in its ability to produce fair outcomes for applicants. On the other hand, when participants discussed the inescapable subjectivity of the law, they emphasised that it could be mastered and employed to achieve substantive justice and correct outcomes; its parameters would provide a 'handy cluster of considerations' to guide the production of fair outcomes for applicants.

With this understanding in place, the next chapter explores the equality orientation of responsive legality – considering in greater detail the way that empowered twenty-first-century administrators' ideal typically blend substantive and procedural concerns in exercising responsive legality.

Notes

1 See Philippe Nonet and Philip Selznick, *Law and Society in Transition: Toward Responsive Law* (Harper, 1978) 79–80, where this is discussed as a core feature of systems of responsive law.
2 The other two studies on bureaucratic legal consciousness are Davina Cooper, 'Local Government Legal Consciousness in the Shadow of Juridification' (1995) 22(4) *Journal of Law and Society* 506–26 and Zach Richards, 'Unearthing Bureaucratic Legal Consciousness: Government Officials' Legal Identification and Moral Ideals' (2015) 11(3) *International Journal of Law in Context* 1–27.
3 Marc Hertogh, 'Through the Eyes of Bureaucrats: How Front-line Officials Understand Administrative Justice' in Michael Adler (ed), *Administrative Justice in Context* (Hart Publishing, 2010) 203–25.
4 Ibid 210.
5 Ibid 212.
6 Ibid 211.
7 Ibid 213.
8 Jerry Mashaw, *Bureaucratic Justice: Managing Social Security Disability Claims* (Yale University Press, 1983).
9 Michael Adler, *Administrative Justice in Context* (Hart Publishing, 2010) 149. See chapter one, 52, of this book.
10 Chris Jewell, *Agents of the Welfare State: How Caseworkers Respond to Need in the United States, Germany and Sweden* (Palgrave Macmillan, 2007).
11 Ibid.
12 Nonet and Selznick, above n 1, 53.
13 Ibid.
14 Ibid 53–70.
15 Ibid 67.
16 David Lieberman, 'Philip Selznick and the Common Law Tradition' in Robert A Kagan, Martin Krygier and Kenneth Winston (eds), *Legality and Community: On the Intellectual Legacy of Philip Selznick* (Littlefield Publishers, 2002) 120.
17 Refer to Chapter 1, page 11, for a detailed discussion.
18 Refer to Chapter 1, pages 10–11, for a detailed discussion.
19 Ibid 91.
20 Refer to Chapter 1, pages 10–11, for a detailed discussion.
21 Nonet and Selznick, above n 1, 108.
22 Refer to Chapter 1, page 16, for a detailed discussion.
23 Ibid.
24 Ibid 111.
25 Ibid 113.
26 See Patricia Ewick and Susan Silbey, *The Common Place of Law* (The University of Chicago Press, 1998) 131.
27 Ibid 132.
28 Sally Engle Merry, *Getting Justice and Getting Even: Legal Consciousness among Working Class Americans* (The University of Chicago Press, 1990).
29 Ibid 143.
30 Ibid.
31 Interview with Anonymous Participant A [SYDNEY AUSTRALIA 8 November 2013].
32 (1989) 169 CLR 379.
33 Interview with [Anonymous Participant E [SYDNEY AUSTRALIA, 10 December 2013].

34 Interview with [Anonymous Participant G], (semi-structured interview) (11 December 2013).
35 Interview with Anonymous Participant B (SYDNEY, AUSTRALIA), 28 November 2013.

Reference list

Articles/books/reports

Adler, Michael, *Administrative Justice in Context* (Hart Publishing, 2010)
Cooper, Davina, 'Local Government Legal Consciousness in the Shadow of Juridification' (1995) 22(4) *Journal of Law and Society* 506
Ewick, Patricia and Susan Silbey, *The Common Place of Law* (The University of Chicago Press, 1998)
Jewell, Chris, *Agents of the Welfare State: How Caseworkers Respond to Need in the United States, Germany and Sweden* (Palgrave MacMillan, 2007)
Kagan, Robert, Martin Krygier and Kenneth Winston, *Legality and Community: On the Intellectual Legacy of Philip Selznick* (Littlefield Publishers, 2002)
Mashaw, Jerry, *Bureaucratic Justice: Managing Social Security Disability Claims* (Yale University Press, 1983)
Merry, Sally Engle, *Getting Justice and Getting Even: Legal Consciousness Among Working Class Americans* (The University of Chicago Press, 1990)
Nonet, Phillippe and Philip Selznick, *Law and Society in Transition: Toward Responsive Law* (Harper, 1978)
Richards, Zach, 'Unearthing Bureaucratic Legal Consciousness: Government Officials' Legal Identification and Moral Ideals' (2015) 11(3) *International Journal of Law in Context*

Case

Chan Yee Kin [1989] 169 CLR 379

Other

Interview with [Anonymous Participant A], (semi-structured interview) (8 November 2013)
Interview with [Anonymous Participant E], (semi-structured interview) (10 December 2013)
Interview with [Anonymous Participant G], (semi-structured interview) (11 December 2013)

4 Equality orientation

Substantive fairness and procedural consistency

Introduction

The equality orientation of responsive legality is a combined striving for substantive fairness and procedural justice. Decision makers justifying their decision according to this type intend for the decision to comply with a range of procedural requirements (be they legal, regulatory or organisational codes and conventions) and also reflect a more individualistic outcomes-based assessment of the unique characteristics and circumstances of the particular matter that might need to be taken into consideration. In other words, decision makers operating according to this type care equally about the outcome of the decision and the process that is followed to achieve that outcome. Though none of the previous socio-legal models of administrative justice notes what I am calling the 'equality orientation' of decision makers operating within the different modes,[1] this new theme is included in the exploration of responsive legality in this book to reflect the importance of this division as discernible as working alongside the other features of the public administration and socio-legal administrative justice literature. This feature of the ideal type is then explored with reference to the RRT officials' discussions in interview, attempting to further tease out the features of a conjoined procedural and substantive justice orientation that is significantly more complex in its duality than the previous models of administrative justice implicitly account for.

Scholarly reflections

Procedural and substantive justice in administrative justice scholarship

Substantive fairness and procedural justice are two interrelated components of justice for citizens, applicants and theorists alike. Where procedural justice, which can be viewed as synonymous with procedural fairness, is concerned with 'process', substantive justice is concerned with outcomes. Procedural fairness is concerned with how individuals are treated and prioritises the importance of treating like individuals the same in like situations, whilst substantive justice focuses on the outcomes that individuals attain.

There have been a number of attempts to specify the requirements of procedural fairness, including, in terms of legal justice, that it requires the right to a fair trial (in the case of criminal prosecutions) and the right to fair proceedings more broadly in relation to civil matters. Whilst there is ongoing debate about the precise dimensions of these requirements, there is wide agreement that in the context of the administrative process like cases should be treated alike, policies should not be applied retrospectively (unless it is to the advantage of the individual concerned to do so), people should be shown respect, their circumstances should be investigated thoroughly, and their claims should be decided impartially and expeditiously regardless of the outcome.

A number of empirical socio-legal studies attest that procedures need not only be valued for the particular outcomes produced, but might also be valued for the general justice done through affording consistent treatment to like individuals. Michael Bayles has argued that values are not derived solely from the dignity and autonomy of individuals but are, drawing on Rawls, what 'rational persons would accept for use in a society in which they are expected to live'.[2] These values include, for example, the values of participation, equal treatment, intelligibility, timeliness and confidence in the decision-making process.[3] Bayles argues that although some of the procedures that give effect to these values may promote accuracy, they should be assessed independently of these effects. Whilst Denis Galligan notes that procedures might also be purposefully valued for the sense in which they lead to correct outcomes, he reiterates Bayles's finding that they are important in and of themselves, as they allow for contextual values to be upheld.

Likewise, Galligan outlines that whilst one sense of fairness consists of achieving outcomes that are required by law, another sense of fairness is linked to these other values and is satisfied when they are respected. He claims that there are authoritative standards based on tiers of values, which constitute the standards of fair treatment, so that a person treated in accordance with them is treated fairly and the procedures are fair to the extent that they have this result. The three tiers consist of the particular area of law that dictates the basic legal objectives that apply, the standards developed in equivalent sources such as common law or policy imperatives and the social principles, which include but go beyond the legal principles. Within this schema, Galligan posits that whilst some standards have an impact on outcomes, directly or indirectly, others place constraints on the course of action that lead to outcomes, and a few are entirely independent of outcomes.

Another influential study was conducted by John Thibaut and Laurens Walker, who studied courtroom litigants' understandings of justice and hypothesised that litigants' satisfaction with dispute resolution outcomes would be independently influenced by their assessment of the fairness of the broader dispute resolution process. They distinguished between process control (control over the opportunity to present evidence) and decision control (control over the final decision) and used experimental methods to test their hypotheses. Their results showed that the method of reaching a decision (i.e. process) and the outcomes these methods generate are both important for individuals to perceive a sense of justice and fairness. Gerald Leventhal devised a subsequent method, which he alleges can be applied to a wide range of non-legal contexts, identifying six justice rules: consistency, bias suppression, accuracy of information, correctability, representation and ethicality. Subsequent empirical research applying Leventhal's model confirmed the importance of four of these notions of justice, specifically suggesting that consistency, accuracy, bias suppression and representation are important underlying dimensions of procedural justice.

More recent studies have since attempted to test the importance of the procedural justice criteria that were derived from the theories of Thibaut and Walker. Tom Tyler set out to test whether Thibaut and Walker's findings were specific to courtroom settings, or whether they could be generalised across other locations outside the courtroom, as well as whether they apply in voluntarily and non-voluntarily pursued situations, and whether the meaning of fairness varies with age, sex, race, education, income and 'liberalism'.[4] Tyler found, through a sample of 652 persons who had previous contact with the police and/or courts, that process and outcome – that is, procedural fairness and substantive justice – were closely related. Amongst other things, he found that in different situations (including where there is voluntary versus involuntary contact and favourable versus unfavourable outcomes) individuals judge the fairness of procedures using different criteria. Interestingly, however, there was no evidence that different types of people judge the fairness of procedures differently. The study is illuminating in its finding that people's perceptions of procedural justice and its importance are clearly complex and multifaceted. Although Tyler's study has been criticised for the artificiality of its initial conceptual separation of procedural and substantive justice and subsequent attempt to empirically study procedural justice only, Adler has convincingly defended Tyler's approach. Adler points out that the models of procedural and substantive justice that inform Tyler's approach are not especially prescriptive and are based on carefully documented empirical research.

In a similar vein to Tyler, this book is conscious of the usefulness of a basic conceptual distinction between procedural and substantive justice, utilising this distinction in its study of administrative officials' understandings of these concepts and how they form part of their normative justification for their decisions.[5]

Furthermore, the new consideration of notions of procedural and substantive justice in the context of government administration is especially called for because the studies on which previous understandings of the division were based were all carried out in the field of criminal justice. Whether they apply to other areas of law – that is, civil and administrative law – has still to be demonstrated. What's more, whilst Adler argues that it is a fundamentally important task to continue to ask whether procedural fairness and substantive justice can be studied in terms of perceptions of those who are subject to official decision making (invoking the maxim 'justice must not only be done but must be seen to be done'),[6] the same can be said for studying these concepts in relation to those responsible for making official decisions. This book, in part, fills this gap, continuing the tradition of studying conceptions of justice in newly called-for combination with consideration of the normative bases on which administrators justify their decisions.

Importing Nonet and Selznick's considerations of procedural and substantive justice

Procedural consistency to avoid repressive governance

Nonet and Selznick begin their analysis of the partial virtues of procedural justice and its relationship with legality or the rule of law with a consideration that legal institutions are themselves inherently scarred, sharing the blemishes of the social order more broadly and serving primarily as tools for exercising power, subsequently favouring the 'haves' over the 'have-nots'.[7] Noting an attack on 'liberal legalism' – an attack on the idea that the pursuits of justice can be served in a supposedly detached, impartial, autonomous system of rules and procedures where 'the rule of law' is unable to cope with the basic issues of social justice and is itself a support for power and privilege – they suggest an alternate view: that law and its corresponding valuation of procedural justice typically upholds a specific kind of order in the form of received moral codes, systems of status and patterns of power. In this, it is far better than the discretionary anarchy afforded in a repressive system of complete rule rejection. It is better than a system where procedural consistency afforded through the impartial application of law is completely rejected; in this case, a problematically primitive system of repressive law and anarchic governance is the result.

Furthermore, in a problematically repressive regime, rampant when procedural justice is rejected in its entirety, a close integration of law and politics results in the form of direct subordination of legal institutions to governing elites. There is also unconstrained official discretion, which is both an outcome and a guarantee of the law's elasticity. Nonet and Selznick conclude that whilst the weakness of repressive law is not necessarily fatal, a regime that indulges the manipulation of law will fail to preserve a foundation of legality and hence that this stage of development is both primitive and dangerous.

In place of this anarchic repressive law – where the decision maker's own personal interests skew the consistent application of the law – Nonet and Selznick outline a more advanced post-repressive system of autonomous law. In this system of autonomous law, the law is, first, separated from politics, whereby the system typically asserts the independence of the judiciary and draws a sharp division between legislative and judicial functions. Second, in autonomous law the legal order promotes a model of rules whereby a focus on these rules helps to enforce official accountability whilst at the same time limiting the creativity of legal institutions and the risk of intrusion into the political domain. Third, and most significant for our discussion here, procedure is seen to be at the heart of law where regularity, rather than substantive justice, is a primary goal of the legal order. That 'procedure is at the heart of law' captures a major strand in the character of autonomous law: the avoidance of repression begins with the growth of a commitment to governance by rules. Procedure, in turn, is the main visible guarantee of the consistent application of rules. In settling disputes among citizens and assessing claims made by or against the state, the legal system offers its most distinctive tool: procedural fairness. In this system, the courts claim expertise as overseers of due process, and integrity of procedure becomes the legal value above all else. Fourth, loyalty to law is understood as strict obedience to the rules of positive law, and criticism of existing laws must be alternatively pursued through the political process. In this model, law is elevated above politics, whereby in interpreting and applying the law the decision maker is to be an objective spokesperson for historically established principles and the obedient allocator of impersonal justice.

Nonet and Selznick outline that one advantage of autonomous law, which has conceptions of procedural justice at its core, is that it is, in principle, judge-centred and rule-bound. This is the case in that, first, rules are an effective resource for legitimating power where they reduce the scope of official authority and thus offer seemingly clear tests of accountability. Second, when judges or other decision makers are perceived as constrained by rules, the apparent range of their discretion is narrowed. Furthermore, an orientation to rules limits the responsibility of the legal system when justice is dispensed in predetermined ways, and in light of fixed obligations and remedies, the legal process can conserve its limited resources.

Considering these strengths, officials justifying their decisions on the basis that they are procedurally consistent might be seen as positively reflecting a step towards the promise of political and social stability that a complete rule of law rejection fails to achieve. In other words, where decisions are justified on the basis of substantive justice alone there is a risk of producing these anarchic consequences that a repressive regime, absent procedural consistency, facilitates.

On the other hand, in discussing the importance of procedural consistency and legality, officials, at times, transcend the limitations of self-serving repressive leadership. In these moments they take a positive step forward, embracing legality and procedural justice for its ability to provide increased governmental stability. In these moments, they are less sensitive to the urgencies of leadership that characterise a poverty of power that often motivates the self-protective manipulation of law, instead striving – on one hand – towards consistent and fair treatment for applicants through the application of generalised and uniform legal principles.

Substantive fairness and procedural justice in responsive legality

It is crucial to note that the equality orientation of responsive legality is a *joint striving* for procedural fairness and substantive justice. Procedural justice, whilst curing many of the ailments of repressive governance, is arbitrary when it frustrates the opportunities for fairness that it strives towards. In the prioritisation of procedural justice alone there is an anxious concern to keep legal reasoning abstract, neutral and unaffected by substantive outcomes where it is believed that result-oriented jurisprudence undermines the integrity of adjudication. Ultimately, within this system of pure procedural justice, decision makers adopt a self-protective and self-limiting stance, and whilst autonomous law demonstrates some desirability in its capacity to restrain the authority of rulers, it narrows the vision of law through the creation of a newly technical spirit with which individuals analyse and interpret the meaning of rules through a highly self-conscious commitment to procedural regularity.

In these moments, where procedural justice is the raison d'être of administrative decision making, officials revert to justifying their decisions on the basis of Mashaw's conception of bureaucratic rationality.[8] In so doing, they demonstrate a strong regard for procedural regularity in union with a new technical spirit, often conservatively emphasising the importance of their own self-protection in these moments. In these utterances, officials revere their own information-processing abilities at the expense of tacitly applying their knowledge or understanding to the problem at hand. One illustration of this with reference to the empirical study was Amanda Jones,[9] who reflects this distinctly technical spirit as she described her role on the tribunal as a specialist in administrative law and someone who is 'proficient in applying complex legislation'. For Jones, it was important that she was a competent administrative lawyer with skills in security law, migration law and planning law, as competency in these areas would allow for correct decisions to be made. Anna Starkos[10] provides another example of this; when presented with a hypothetical claim of an Afghani applicant and asked how she would assess the claim, Starkos responded that she would rely on the *Refugee Convention* to determine the outcome and would systematically work her way through the difficult terms of the *Convention* to come to a correct answer. In these moments where the law was perceived as a body of difficult and dense rational rules to be skilfully applied by intelligent decision makers, officials perpetuated a Weberian, or Mashawian, understanding of bureaucratic rationality, believing that formalistic and rational rules are to be applied in the pursuit of their own efficient administration.

It is not only Nonet and Selznick who emphasise the importance of a substantive justice-oriented system of responsive law, as discussed in the previous chapter. Purpose-driven responsive law has also been a continuing preoccupation of modern legal theory; as Jerome Frank has noted, a core purpose of a number of legal theorists has been to make law 'more responsive to social needs'.[11] When Lon Fuller discusses the centrality of purpose in the legal enterprise,[12] for example, or when Ronald Dworkin considers the importance of principle and policy as foundations of legal reasoning,[13] they reflect the modern aspiration for a legal order that is effective in dealing with change.

On this view, good law should offer something in addition to procedural justice. Law should be competent and fair at the same time in that it should define the public interest and be committed to the achievement of substantive justice. In this prioritisation of responsive law, legal institutions are required to surrender the inward-looking safety of autonomous law and become instruments of social ordering and social change, such that activism, openness and cognitive competence begin to emerge.

The critical step in this transition from autonomous to responsive law is the generalisation of law's objectives where particular rules, policies and procedures begin to be regarded as instrumental and expendable. The emphasis shifts to general goals, and there is a new search for the implicit values inherent in rules and policies. In this process, the generalisation of purpose is a core source of flexibility within the modern organisation. It is this flexibility and complexity that should be accounted for in recognising and applauding the dual procedural and substantive justice orientation of responsive legality and explicitly importing this duality into the socio-legal models of administrative justice. On the other hand, traditional bureaucracy is criticised for its tendency to transform means – encompassing rules and operational objectives – into ends. Responsive law therefore builds on the limitations of autonomous law in that it looks for purpose in the elaboration of rules and recognises that if rules are to be applied with precision, events must be classified accurately. This is an important development from autonomous law because rules necessarily depend for their relevance and role on the viability of appropriate historical conditions; as circumstances change, rules must be refashioned both to protect the needs of policy and to protect the authority of the rules themselves. As such, particular guidance is drawn from authoritative principles such as concepts of fairness, democracy, or the idea that no one should profit from his own wrong.

However, as briefly explored in the previous chapter, one critique of this form of law and governance is that it may weaken the consistency of procedure and allow citizens to more easily do as they wish. The criticism is that the law then loses its capacity to properly restrain individuals and command obedience. On this view, unaccountable discretion is alien to legal ordering because decision makers can act out according to their whims, making consistency of treatment subject to a shifting political climate.

Within this blend of strengths and shortcomings, the primary advantage of purposive-oriented decision making that blends procedural and substantive concerns is that, in its emphasis on principle, it is a rich resource for criticising the authority of specific rules. Under this model, whilst a rule might meet the official criteria for legal validity, it should also be helpfully reassessed in light of its consequences for the values that are at stake. This might remind us of Frank Grey's discussion of the trivial laws regarding letters in the RRT needing to be addressed directly to applicants, such that even if they, in fact, reached the correct applicant, their incorrect salutation would cause them to be sent back on jurisdictional error.[14] Or it is also epitomised by another applicant, John Simpson, who discussed a line of cases regarding the relevance of an applicant writing home to their family as a measure for assessing the believability of their claims and the absurdity of these rules given the limited tendency for individuals to write letters in the contemporary day.[15] As Nonet and Selznick discuss, an emphasis on purpose and context, like that emphasised by Simpson and Grey, helpfully enhances rationality in legal reasoning, though the increase of purposiveness in law means that it becomes increasingly difficult to distinguish legal analysis from policy analysis and legal rationality from other forms of systematic decision making. However, with this opportunity cost, purposive legal thought also reduces the tendency for officials to retreat behind specific rules and escape responsibility. For purpose to gain authority, law must be able to elaborate the mandates of legal institutions, such that a critical phase of responsive law is the definition of mission, or, the transformation of general purpose into specific objectives. In this sense, purposiveness requires inquiry into substantive outcomes and the consideration of what is factually needed to effectually realise institutional responsibilities. Otherwise put, purposive law is result-oriented, significantly departing from an emphasis on procedural justice in autonomous law, which is ignorant of consequences.

Empirical reflections in the RRT

Valuations of procedural and substantive justice in responsive legality

There were many times when RRT participants reflected a sincere regard for procedural and substantive justice simultaneously – in these moments reflecting the dual aspects of the responsive-legality type.

One participant who at times reflected these dual features of the type was Amanda Jones.[16] Jones was a high-profile legal personality who had worked in a number of senior legal roles. She had worked as a judge on a variety of administrative tribunals after completing her law degree and practical legal training many years earlier. Jones recurrently emphasised the importance of the law – describing that she began work on the RRT so that she could put her well-developed legal skills to good use. She discussed that she had only ever described herself as

> [a]n administrative lawyer who has skills in interpreting and applying complex legislation. So I have always taken the view that I am able to become sufficiently competent in social security law, and migration law, and planning law, to be a good decision maker in those areas.

In these moments, the law allowed Jones to exercise her analytical abilities and provided a framework for reasoned decision making. Jones reflected at one point,

> Can I say to you I think it is far better for a member to have a legal background in general, or at least those analytical and reasoning skills that we learn as lawyers. And it is better for them to understand the statute, interpretation, understand case law or whatever. In my experience there are some non-lawyers who have it, but it is those analytical skills that matter.

For Jones, these analytical skills are to be consistently drawn on in the application of the law so that consistent treatment can be afforded to all individuals, again presenting visions of administrative justice as tied to the delivery of consistent procedure. Jones reflected,

> I'm probably the – how should I put it? – the resident therapeutic jurisprude. And it was when I first heard about TJ [therapeutic jurisprudence], with

> David Wexler and Bruce Winick giving it that name, I thought 'gee, this is what I and a number of other people have always practised'. So first I came across the term more than a decade ago, and that's my principle: that win or lose, I want to make people feel that they've had the opportunity to say everything that they wanted to say and not cut them off . . . so, with the TJ, I think I've always done that – and it's treating people with dignity and respect and hearing what their story is.

Here, Jones reflected that the correct outcome is closely tied to the way that the applicant is treated in the hearing. For Jones, a good outcome would (at least in part) be attained if all applicants were treated with fairness and respect.

Like Jones, Rebecca Yii[17] also viewed the law as an important guide for the necessary production of procedural justice for the applicant. For Yii, this production of procedural justice would simultaneously assist in achieving good outcomes and an overall sense of fairness for the individual applicant. Yii had spent many years working for government before taking up her position on the RRT. Not coming from a legal background but having studied politics at university, she said that she took up the position on the tribunal so that she could 'expand her legal skills' and 'apply her experience in government to a worthwhile role'. Yii reflected this conjoined valuation of legality and meaningful or worthwhile government decision making throughout her more specific reflections on her 11 years working at the RRT, recurrently discussing the ways that the law equipped her to make fair decisions through providing consistent and impartial treatment to applicants. For Yii, the law provided an important and informative set of provisions for achieving procedural fairness, as it required decision makers to be transparent to applicants about their case in order to give them the best possible chance of meeting any opposition that the decision maker might have to their claim. For Yii, it was unacceptable that members would withhold information from the applicant as natural justice was in these moments denied; inconsistent procedure through the failure to follow procedural legal provisions meant that justice was not obtained. Yii outlined this further:

> I can remember, and this is gossip more than anything and I know you're taping but I wouldn't deny it anyway . . . I was downstairs when applicants were at the counter or on the phone absolutely bawling their eyes out because they [had] understood that they were going to get a favourable decision from the member. Because they didn't understand. Because nobody had explained to them very quickly what was required and what was the consequence of what was said – they didn't explain what was the effect of what they said.

In these moments, Yii expressed a clear disregard for decision makers who did not openly disclose information about how they were assessing the applicant's claims, expressing that this was unfair for applicants in that they were denied natural justice in the process. This denial was closely paralleled for Yii with a disregard for the guiding parameters of the law and a hesitancy in explicitly citing and following the law and making the legal framework clearly known to applicants. Yii further outlined this:

> Well, if you find out what they've said [and] then that means that [they] weren't there, [you might say to them] 'this indicates strongly to me that the dates that you've given in this statement are in complete contrast to what you told me in the hearing; therefore, that might establish to me that you couldn't have been arrested and you couldn't have been tortured; therefore I can't find that for political reasons you are being persecuted; therefore you are not going to come under the *Convention*'.

As Yii discussed earlier, the law functioned in these moments as a framework for the decision maker that should be relayed to the applicant to inform them of their likelihood of success. This transparency and consistency in treatment through applying and informatively disclosing the law provided the key to assuring that natural justice was done for the applicant. Yii went on to say,

> You have that responsibility, particularly during the oral, oh 349 or whatever it's called, where you have to say 'look, if there is some *adverse information* then you need to get it in writing; you can request an extension of time', you know, all of that stuff. So you need to clearly explain that if you are going to allow . . . but even if it didn't come to that and there wasn't that requirement to put that *adverse information* . . . even if it was leading to a different conclusion, I think you need to explain that 'these are all the things that I have some issues with'. And it was always quicker to put that *information* at a hearing and explain it clearly, but sometimes I'd write a letter anyway. Because it is better doing an abundance of natural justice than it is doing too little.

In truth, at many times these participants reflected aspects of Adler's legal type (in their emphasis on legality) or Mashaw's moral judgement (in their emphasis on fairness, in general), but it was at those moments when the two fused together that they reflected features of the more nuanced responsive-legality type.

In this, the explicit emphasis on the dual equality orientation of valuing procedural and substantive justice is an important and admirable feature of responsive legality, where public officials and organisations can be celebrated – when justifying their decision on this basis – for adopting a comparatively selfless range of normative concerns necessary for driving administrative justice forward.

Notes

1 Refer back to Chapter 1, pages 8–15, for a detailed discussion of these models.
2 Michael Bayles, *Procedural Justice: Allocating to Individuals* (Kluwer Academic Publishers, 1990) 11.
3 Ibid.

4 Ibid.
5 Note that the empirical research informing the findings in this study was by no means prescriptive in scope. Participants were not even asked explicitly to reflect on their attitudes towards justice; instead, the interview conversations naturally and organically revealed varying conceptions of procedural and substantive justice, which were, unlike in Tyler's study, concepts that revealed themselves retrospectively from the data without any initial consideration of them before the interviews progressed. As discussed at greater length in Chapters 5, 6 and 7, a similarly useful and noteworthy distinction between the emphasis on procedural and substantive justice that was pioneered by Tyler in relation to those using the legal system can newly be observed in relation to those exerting some degree of control over the operations of the legal system (i.e. the bureaucratic decision makers responsible for implementing the law and achieving the operationalisation of conceptions of justice).
6 Ibid.
7 Philippe Nonet and Philip Selznick, *Law and Society in Transition: Toward Responsive Law* (Harper, 1978) 4.
8 Refer back to Chapter 1, pages 8–10, for a detailed discussion.
9 Interview with [Anonymous Participant D], (semi-structured interview) (3 December 2013).
10 Interview with [Anonymous Participant C], (semi-structured interview) (3 December 2013).
11 Jerome Frank, 'Mr Justice Holmes and Non-Euclidian Legal Thinking' (1932) 17 *Cornell Law Quarterly* 568, 586 cited in Nonet and Selznick, above n 36, 73.
12 Lon Fuller, 'Positivism and Fidelity to Law – A Reply to Professor Hart' (1958) 71 *Harvard Law Review* 630, 667 cited in Nonet and Selznick, above n 36, 81.
13 Ronald Dworkin, 'The Model of Rules' (1967) 35 *University of Chicago Law Review* 14 cited in Nonet and Selznick, above n 36, 81.
14 Refer to pages 99–100 of this book.
15 Refer to page 96 of this book.
16 Interview with [Anonymous Participant D], (semi-structured interview) (3 December 2013).
17 Interview with [Anonymous Participant Z], (semi-structured interview) (30 January 2014).

Reference list

Articles/books/reports

Bayles, Michael, *Procedural Justice: Allocating to Individuals* (Kluwer Academic Publishers, 1990)

Nonet, Philippe and Philip Selznick, *Law and Society in Transition: Toward Responsive Law* (Harper, 1978)

Other

Interview with [Anonymous Participant C], (semi-structured interview) (3 December 2013)

Interview with [Anonymous Participant D], (semi-structured interview) (3 December 2013)

Interview with [Anonymous Participant Z], (semi-structured interview) (30 January 2014)

5 Cognitive techniques

Applying experience and verifying the truth

Introduction

This chapter argues that the cognitive techniques drawn on in the responsive legality ideal type are the application of experience and verification of truth – and positively so. Decision makers justifying their decisions according to this type draw on their personal experience in a range of contexts to apply relevant and contextually specific knowledge and discernment to the task at hand. In this sense, they understand, whether explicitly or subconsciously, the importance of tacit (or experientially based) knowledge and the difference between data, information and knowledge that sets tacit knowledge users apart from those who apply more superficial stand-alone recitations of information. Whilst data consist of raw facts and information is the collection of facts themselves, experientially formed knowledge is the body of rules, guidelines and procedures used to select, organise and manipulate data to make it suitable for a specific task.[1] Decision makers working to protect applicant welfare through rule-of-law compliance – demonstrating a drive towards responsiveness and dual valuation of procedural and substantive fairness – embody the responsive-legality type when they also apply their tacit knowledge, acquired through personal experiences, to their decision making. This chapter argues that in doing so, they are better able to perceive the factual truth of a situation and, accordingly, better able to understand how to apply laws, rules, judgements, perceptions and intuitions to the unique matter at hand.

Scholarly reflections

Tacit knowledge valuation

Whilst explicit knowledge and tacit knowledge are both important features of knowledge management (KM), tacit knowledge sits at the very heart of KM, and is the crucial component for spreading knowledge throughout organisations and instigating organisational innovation. Whilst explicit knowledge has been described as a 'surface pool that is easier to detect and capture, but which represents only a fraction of organisational knowledge',[2] tacit knowledge has been theorised as a 'deep, buried reserve'[3] that is embedded in an individual's ideas, insights, values and judgements.

From the perspective of the organisation and public office, there are multiple benefits to valuing tacit knowledge: benefits that a valuation of explicit knowledge alone misses. The knowledge management literature has also drawn attention to the ways that experiential knowledge has been shown to be central to organisational decision making – suggesting that it is commonplace for decision makers to justify their decisions through directly applying the knowledge that has been tacitly, rather than formally, learnt through a range of broad life experiences.

Tacit knowledge has been found to be the cornerstone of true knowledge dispersal across a number of contemporary organisations. Michelle Martinez outlines that tacit knowledge management reaches to the heart of 'encouraging individuals to communicate their knowledge by creating environments and systems for capturing, organising, and sharing knowledge'[4] throughout the organisation. Peter Clark, Chris Carter and Isabelle Szmigin have pointed out that far too often, knowledge management has been narrowly and incorrectly perceived to revolve around the codification of knowledge. In fact, as multiple studies have found, 90 per cent of organisational knowledge is tacitly embedded and created in the minds of staff.[5]

Another reason why tacit knowledge is crucial to organisational knowledge management is that it is importantly attuned to the quotidian aspects of culture that explicit knowledge ignores. Kaj Koskinen, for example, finds that in Finland, much organisation-based tacit knowledge is transferred in the male/female separated saunas, which makes knowledge transmittance across the sexes in the boardroom difficult. There are even further complexities when it comes to modern Western organisations, such as the RRT context empirically studied here, in that there are additional needs in such contexts to integrate the tacit knowledge background of its (often) highly multicultural staff because

> cross cultural working involves the interaction of people whose tacit knowledge has been developed in different ways and who have learnt different approaches to sense reading and sense giving.[6]

Whilst a complete nationality profile of the interviewed RRT participants in this study was not taken, the open-ended interviews revealed that participants came from a diverse range of ethnic backgrounds: India, China, Argentina, Brazil, the US, Somalia, Chile, England and Australia, to name a few. In this sense, the participants reflected the diverse demographic make-up of modern Western administrative organisations that Koskinen emphasises is a crucial cultural aspect that makes tacit knowledge diffusion central to effective knowledge management. Walshman has made a similar argument in a study comparing British and Japanese engineers where the two nationalities of engineers were forced to work together to examine their approaches to tacit knowledge. It was found that whilst distrustful at first of each other's approaches to design tasks, the formalised British soon came to appreciate the Japanese approach to multifunctional teams, permitting a far greater degree of tacit flow between team members. Similarly, Busch's study of tacit knowledge dissemination in three information technology (IT) firms emphasised that the multicultural nature of organisation X, with more than 50 IT staff members (out of 108) speaking more than 35 languages other than English, added to the central importance of tacit knowledge within this space.

Where officials differ markedly in many aspects of their socialisation, beliefs, culture and language orientation, tacit knowledge – what we know makes up 90 per cent of organisational knowledge – is highly complex and multifaceted, deriving from a range of cross-cultural sources that must be harnessed and appreciated in order for understandings of what constitutes knowledge in the organisation to be captured.

The importance of tacit knowledge to understandings of knowledge operations in government administration also rests in the epistemological truth that where there are humans, the very roots of knowledge are tacit. Government bureaucracy is not operated by robotic machines but by cognisant individuals. As Jacob and Ebrahimpur outline, 'software may be appropriate for information transfer, but individuals are generally considered appropriate for "knowledge" transfer'.[7] It is important here to recognise that knowledge exists as part of a holistic system, where

> knowledge is not a thing in, and of, itself, but is rather a bundle or network of various elements: bodies, machines, communications technologies, and materials of all sorts . . . no one has ever observed a fact, a theory, or a machine that could survive outside of the networks that gave birth to them. Still more fragile than termites, facts and machines can travel along extended galleries, but they cannot survive one minute in this famous and mythical 'out-thereness' so vaunted by philosophers of science.[8]

Add to this the finding that knowledge is communicated largely informally. It was found in a survey of 97 UK firms, for example, that a large majority of tacit knowledge is communicated through informal meetings, whereas a substantially smaller amount had been acquired through formal discussion.[9] The study also found that the lessons that were learnt at work were largely passed on through discussion groups, rather than through presentations. On the micro-organisational level, Daft and Lengel found that there exists a five-step knowledge transfer continuum comprising of (1) face-to-face interaction, (2) the telephone, (3) written personal communication, (4) written formal communication and (5) numerical formal communication.[10]

Such findings are mirrored in the large stores of knowledge missed by those interviewed RRT participants who idealised the role of explicit codified knowledge in their decision making. Reference to particular legal regulations, codes and provisions and formalised modes of learning were ignorant of the vast bulk of informal types of knowledge material and transfer that underpinned this codified knowledge. Such findings regarding the importance of tacit knowledge transmittance through non-formal means also bolster the reliability and validity of the open-ended interview format conducted with RRT members, where the empirical findings that were generated would, of course, not have been extrapolated through the analysis of explicit legal decisions, written records or formalised meetings with RRT staff. Rather, the most flexible and informal approach to studying these officials was pursued to generate broad and deep understandings of these individuals' normative justice leanings and thus generate more than mere information in the pursuance of knowledge.

As the organisational studies in KM literature have extensively found, there are numerous and profound ways that tacit knowledge is spread across contemporary organisations, whereby officials draw on their experientially formed tacit knowledge to justify their decisions. As these studies show, tacit knowledge across organisations is the most effective means for true knowledge dispersal, it acknowledges hidden aspects of culture that a valuation of explicit knowledge alone misses, it appreciates the epistemological foundations of knowledge as rooted in human networks and it thrives on the informality that makes real knowledge transfer possible. Together these studies attest that tacit knowledge is becoming increasingly important in organisational operations.

Whilst at some moments officials value explicit codified knowledge – aligning in these moments most closely with Mashaw's bureaucratic rationality in the rigid application of information processing as the core cognitive technique[11] – at other times, when justifying their decisions in accordance with the responsive-legality type, officials embody the belief that true knowledge rests in the informal, experiential 'deep, buried reserves' that drive the decision maker's ideas, insights, values and judgements.

Contextualised truth claims

Apart from applying their experiential tacit knowledge, decision makers also emphasised the importance of verifying the truth in close accord with their valuation of responsiveness and achieving applicant welfare through dual applications of substantive and procedural justice – together embodying the responsive-legality type.

There are interesting overlaps here with Mashaw's work, [12] where crucial to Mashaw's normative arguments about bureaucratic justice is the finding that whilst information-processing pursuits strive towards the attainment of bureaucratic rationality, such rationality attainment is, in fact, a logical impossibility. It fails to produce the system goals it strives towards at the expense of even beginning to achieve broader bureaucratic goals such as substantive justice.

Indeed, there are multiple general limits on achieving rational decision making in bureaucracy, including, as Mashaw found, limitations in bureaucratic cognitive competence and communication problems within the organisation. Mashaw outlines that individuals within organisations can neither faultlessly collect and process all the information that is relevant to the decision that they made nor possibly process information in an objective and entirely accurate manner. A pure model of instrumental rationality that relies on information processing as its cognitive mode must therefore presume that the values or reference goals for decision making are absolute (i.e, that the choice of one goal over another is not morally distressing) and that they are relevant, stable, consistent, precise and exogenous. To the contrary, Mashaw finds that social policy applied within legislation within bureaucracy, and interpreted and applied by administrative officials, does not provide fully coherent approaches to unitary goals and that 'it will always be possible to find that from the perspective of one or another goal that the administrator's actions are instrumentally irrational'. [13]

Importing Mashaw's holistic findings to the present context, we can similarly note the impossibility of individual administrators producing the system goals of rationalisation where information processing is the core cognitive technique that they apply. As Mashaw finds, attempts to process information become lost in a human organisation, where what begins as a reflective question, 'What about X?' becomes, first, 'do X' and, then, 'X is imperative', disabling the individual from correctly evaluating information and coming to any kind of rational decision on the basis that mixed messages are sent. Such findings are certainly not limited to Mashaw's work; as Mashaw acknowledges, the notion that instrumental rationality in its pure form is unachievable is not 'headline news';[14] in fact, the exploration of the difficulties of implementation of rationality within bureaucracy has become a field of policy studies in and of itself. But epitomising the findings in the field, Mashaw's study can alert us to the pitfalls of officials idealising and pursuing information processing in their decision making, as such pursuit can never achieve the system goals of bureaucratic rationality that they strive for.

In addition to this ironic irrationality, Mashaw outlines that the rational administration of public administration comes at a cost – that is, it comes at the opportunity cost of pursuing other social goals. For broader conceptions of substantive justice and considerations of the welfare of the applicant to be pursued, rational administration cannot drive the administration's operations.

Empirical reflections in the RRT

Experience/tacit knowledge and truth verification valuation in the RRT

A number of participant officials provided rich accounts of tacit knowledge and truth verification valuation in close accord with the previously discussed components of the responsive legality ideal type. To illustrate the uniformity between the various conceptual features of the type, there is some repetition in the use of these examples – so that it is clear for readers how the previously discussed elements of the ideal type also require tacit knowledge valuation for their identification as responsive legality. We might take the example of Cate Arnolds to illustrate.[15] As previously discussed, Arnolds had worked in a number of legal roles before beginning on the tribunal, including having worked in a legal capacity for government and in a number of human rights organisations. However, for Arnolds, quite apart from exercising her legal skills, the most rewarding aspect of working on the tribunal was the moment when she 'discovered' her first refugee. She recounts that when this happened: 'I went away and had a little cry, actually'. She prided herself in her ability to empathise with the applicants and to get to the bottom of their stories to ascertain the genuineness of the claims that were presented. She gave the example of an applicant who had been a filmmaker in Iran who initially presented a somewhat confusing story in the hearing. Arnolds was concerned that this applicant was unable to express his story in a way that would meet the legal criteria and that underneath there was a 'real and genuine' story. Her solution, learnt through her experience working in human rights organisations with vulnerable applicants, was to tell the applicant to go away and to return to the hearing in a week's time when they were both thinking more clearly so that she could 'get everything straight'.

For Arnolds, it was incredibly important when conducting tribunal decision making to be able to empathise with people, and 'if you didn't have experience of some sort, I think you would struggle'. Arnolds went on, saying,

> Having said that, there were people there who were very much black letter lawyers who were there and um they had their own hired hand to do things. It's not how I would have approached things, you know, there were some people who didn't do well and I just don't know how they would have coped. I think you have to have a degree of empathy that comes from, you know, life experiences from people who had various experiences in life umm yes and whether that comes through travel or volunteering in various areas or whatever.

Arnolds reflected that 'black letter lawyers' lacked the empathy required for good decision making, which comes instead through personal experiences such as travel or volunteering. For Arnolds, despite having a thorough knowledge of and experience with the law, the law alone did not provide the skills required to be a good decision maker as far as attaining the important goal of substantive justice for applicants was concerned. The ability to achieve correct outcomes for applicants, as for her Iranian filmmaker, came instead through the broader capacity to empathise, instilled through life experience.

Like Arnolds, Julie Miller[16] constructed a vision of a law incapable, on its own, of empathising with applicants and falling short of achieving substantive justice in terms of fair outcomes. Miller's background was in the medical field rather than law. She had been a nurse for many years before beginning on the tribunal. Between reflecting on her nursing training, raising children and experiencing hard relationships with violent men, Miller expressed a belief in the importance of care and empathy that was gained through personal experience and struggle, which the law alone could not fully capture. Miller spoke about issues of bias confrontation that she had previously learnt in the medical field and that she believed were lacking in practice in the 'legalistic' RRT environment. She discussed her former experiences in the sexual health field, recounting that she was encouraged to be open-minded towards gay HIV patients often from illicit sexual backgrounds.

She discussed the way that she was initially unable to understand or respect these individuals, but through exposure over time she became more able to put herself in their shoes. When asked whether an understanding of the law facilitated better RRT decision making, Miller asserted that it did not. She recurrently referred to her personal experience and the empathy that it gave her, claiming that these life experiences were crucial for understanding and appreciating applicants in order to achieve substantive justice through fair outcomes, which was not achievable through the application of a callous law.

Embodying this further is John Simpson.[17] Simpson was a professor of law who had occupied many senior academic roles in Australian universities. He had extensive research and teaching experience and, apart from his prominent role in academia, had also filled numerous other legal and human rights positions before taking a part-time post on the tribunal. Simpson had also travelled widely and spent much of his life living in other countries, especially a number of countries across Africa. Simpson recurrently reflected a clear regard for life experience and substantive individualised justice simultaneously. His decision making was driven by an idealisation of the role of cultural awareness gained through personal experience that codified knowledge itself could not clearly express.

Simpson saw the tribunal as a practical forum where his rich experience could make a real difference to people's lives in a dynamic setting. He reflected that he took up the position on the tribunal because 'what's missing in academia is of course what I describe as a "practical angle" to specific issues, especially in international law'. He claimed,

> I took the view, for instance, that for a student in the classroom nothing is much more exciting than having a lecturer, a Professor, who has participated in a particular case coming to the classroom to talk about their experience in the wider context and their experience in the particular context in dealing with a particular issue. Here you are not talking about a book; you are not talking about theories – you are talking about how books and theories come together to work in practice. It is what academia lacks. I took up this job with that urgent desire: that I would like to teach refugee law from a certain perspective, not just from the perspective of theory but telling them what really happens when you present your case; what is expected; what is looked at; and what are some of the legal and other factors that shape the decision-making process which eventually becomes what we read in the reports. I was very keen on that.

At one point Simpson reflected that his international travel and living experience 'equipped [him] to understand' the live issues in a case in a way that an understanding of the explicit law could not. He reflected that meeting someone from Afghanistan in one moment, Somalia the next, and Mali the next – which he described as a common occurrence when living in Africa – gives one a 'rich tapestry of human connection' which means that you are 'equipped to understand'. For Simpson, such experience meant that 'you have a sense of humanity, which allows you to assess what someone is telling you'. In his emphasis on individualised substantive justice, he expressed remorse for unsuccessful applicants who were caught out as a result of the experience of the decision maker, which he alleged makes them more perceptive and able to correctly determine issues of credibility. Despite this remorse, however, he saw the correct determination of applicant credibility as crucial to achieving broader visions of administrative justice, whereby he believed that the applicant's situation would be correctly assessed by the discerning and worldly decision maker.

Simpson discussed that if you had done a diplomatic post in Nigeria or Ghana or Somalia, for example, or in many areas of the European world, and if an applicant is talking about the conditions in that country, then the decision maker is likely to know about those conditions and to assess the truthfulness of those claims. For Simpson, 'this is a very difficult situation to explain and the law doesn't show that'. In trying to illustrate this 'difficult to explain' situation, Simpson gave the example of a situation where a decision maker asked the applicant if they had been writing home to their family, discussing a line of cases where the decision makers suggest that applicants claiming to still have family at home would presumably be writing home if they are telling the truth about having been persecuted in their country of origin. Simpson pointed out that if this decision maker followed that line of cases, they might ask the applicant, 'Have you been writing letters home?' He said, however, that the truth is that 'these days nobody writes letters. They write emails or use phone cards to call home, but the system is such that you are forced to ask them about letters and so they pretend that they write letters'. He cynically summarised that 'it doesn't make sense. Now the refugee system pushes them to shape their stories to fit the template. It's a sad reality. Somehow your background equips you better'.

Simpson's cynicism towards the limitations for applying explicit knowledge to produce substantive justice was shared by Afif Hamid,[18] who also discussed the profound importance of applying the life lessons one learns through personal experience to good decision making. For Hamid, the review courts were unrealistic about the facts, and whilst he diplomatically asserted, 'I have to be careful what I say here', his recurrent cynicism reflected an unyielding belief that rule-based law was limited in its ability to produce good decision making and to reflect the more advanced cultural awareness that a decision maker might instead obtain through other life experience. He went on to say that

> the courts have one view of the law . . . and the considerations by the courts are often related to the black letter details of the law, whereas the environment in which we make our decisions is anything but that.

Like Simpson seeking to escape a theory-bound teaching environment and gain practical experience to bring to his students in representing the law, Hamid reflected on the manner in which he would seek to immerse himself in the culture of the RRT and draw on other people's experiences as a mechanism for deciding claims. He discussed that he would draw on other people's rich cultural experience and understandings to come to correct decisions, which was 'not achievable in the straightforward application of the rule-bound law'. Again diplomatically, Hamid asserted, 'I don't want to demean the profession, but sometimes I'm just saying that more basic instincts come out than the law', and in these moments it was these more basic instincts, tacitly formed, that produced the basis for the decision.

Like Hamid, Justine Anderson[19] also expressed a preference for adopting the values learnt through personal experience, rather than codified knowledge, to produce good decisions that accurately ascertained the truthfulness of the claim. Anderson had worked in family law for many years before beginning on the tribunal and explained that she came upon the position at the RRT 'by chance' when a friend of hers saw the advertisement in the paper and recommended that she apply. She recounted the lengthy time it would take to write a decision, the various structural and administrative changes that the tribunal had undergone over the years and the onerous requirements to give notice to applicants before affirming their case. In these accounts, Anderson offered that

> [t]here is a range of elements to fair decision making that is not just about how to apply the law. In the narrow sense, applying the law is all about being a fair decision maker, so many non-legal members were very, very good members because they weren't constrained by technical legal aspects but they were just fair, decent human beings with some life experience who were able to effectively interact with the claimant and hear them fairly and come to a reasonable decision about what the claims were.

In these moments individuals discussed, like Ewick and Silbey's citizens, the way that law was unable to deal with the recurrent problems of everyday life. Ewick and Silbey explain that for their citizen participants, images of legality in these moments are 'mired in formal procedure, captured by bureaucratic structures and remote from the real concerns of citizens. . .'.[20] For these individuals, 'the law is unable to effectively resolve disputes, recognise truth, or respond to injustice'.[21] Ewick and Silbey's respondents discussed that the law was powerful but ineffective, creating barriers that ordinary people could not surmount. For bureaucrats studied here, on the other side of the decision-making process, the law was similarly counterproductive in the production of justice; it was a constraining force that at times prevented the correct outcome from being made. Explicit codified knowledge lacked the decency that personal experience would provide to these decision makers, which would allow them to effectively engage with the claimant and come to a reasonable decision.

Tacit knowledge, substantive justice and the responsive-legality type

As explored throughout the previous chapters, responsive legality is only present where each of its features arise simultaneously. As such, responsive legality is more complex in terms of its equality orientation than each of the pre-existing models of administrative justice in that it combines a dual emphasis on procedural and substantive justice. And as Chapter 3 explored, the legitimating value of responsive legality was different from other models of administrative justice in that the core goal for the decision maker was to behave adaptively and flexibly to changed conditions; purposively moving within the parameters of the law to meet applicant needs. This section further explores the uniqueness, and some of the strengths, of the responsive-legality type through the consideration of an alternate situation where decision makers justify their decisions through the application of 'information processing' as the core cognitive technique (as in Mashaw's bureaucratic rationality) and commonly fail to consider the substantive justice of the applicant in this process. As the knowledge management literature has revealed, this creates knowledge transmittance impediments for the organisation. It also problematically shifts the decision making emphasis off the production of substantive justice for the applicant, and onto administrative self-preservation and protection from judicial review for the decision maker.

At many points in the interview conversations, those who idealised explicit knowledge and information processing simultaneously emphasised the importance of using this knowledge to protect their decision against review by the courts. Considerations of substantive justice and the outcome for the applicant were entirely missing from these accounts. For example, for one participant demonstrating recurrently high legal identification and recurrent regard for explicit legal knowledge reflected that

> there are a couple of things with decision making. One is whether or not you are trying to, you are conscious of the fact that your decisions are reviewable on judicial review grounds. I would say that people with law degrees should have a really clear understanding of what jurisdictional error is.[22]

She elaborated that making a good refugee credibility assessment was dependent on the decision maker having a clear understanding of what jurisdictional error is so that they would be 'kept safe from any claim of apprehended bias and pre-judgments'.

In contrast to these concurrent expressions of high regard for explicit legal knowledge and concern for protection against judicial review, expressions of high regard for experiential tacit knowledge reflected a simultaneous scepticism for the self-preserving goals of protecting against judicial review, which was replaced with an overriding concern for the welfare of the applicant.

This is epitomised by Frank Grey, who claimed,

> I think it is demonstrable if one looks at the record, where it is arguable that the wrong decision has been made on a particular case; on any particular case, it's almost invariably because of a misunderstanding or mistaken analysis of the facts of a claimant's case and not because of a mistake in the application of the law. Now when I say a 'wrong decision' I don't mean an 'unlawful decision', because jurisdictional error of course is quite uncommon . . . when I was on the RRT about 5% of RRT decisions were overturned by the

> Federal Magistrates Court, or the Federal Court, which is not a very high proportion.[23]

Here, Grey distinguishes between the explicit, codified legal knowledge involved in making refugee credibility assessments – which he identifies as of minor importance, recounting that jurisdictional error is open only on a limited number of grounds and that only 5 per cent of decisions are appealed to the courts for legal points – and the more crucial factual assessment, which he identifies as paramount on the basis that an applicant's fate turns on the outcome where courts cannot intervene to alter understandings of the facts and the decision of the tribunal is final. He goes on to provide an example of the centrality of tacit understandings of culture and place to conducting refugee credibility assessments that produce substantive justice, with regards to the Hazaras from Afghanistan.

Grey recounts that Hazaras from the district of Jaghori in the province of Ghazni in Afghanistan are thought by members to live in a province that is overwhelmingly peaceful and that claims of persecution from this region are therefore commonly denied on the basis that applicants can return to that place without fear of persecution. He claims, however, that if one 'thinks outside the box' and tacitly contextualises this information, the truth is that Jaghori is two-thirds the size of the Australian Capital Territory in a country about two-thirds the size of New South Wales and is a very small and poor district with no employment prospects. He says that if you send a man back, he might house his family in Jaghori, but he is still going to have to go back to Kabul or somewhere else just to find work, which means travelling outside Jaghori where all roads are interdicted by the Taliban. He questions then,

> What does it mean to say that you can go to Jaghori? It's impractical. And in my view quite stupid, which is why when I was a reviewer I never gave that a second thought. I mean if the only suggestion that a departmental officer had is that 'this person could go back to Jaghori', then as a reviewer I would send the thing back to the department and say 'give him a visa because this is silly'.

When summarising what skills were important to making this assessment, Grey claimed that 'you need to have the capacity to understand foreign countries; foreign cultures'. And when it was put to him that members with developed explicit knowledge of the codified law were able to write better with the audience of the courts in mind and protect against jurisdictional error, he responded 'Yeah, but they're still wrong'. He went on to summarise what he saw as the absurdity of decisions that did not accurately understand the truth of the living conditions and circumstances of individuals in their home country through reference to a Federal Court judgement where the judge quoted,

> If the Commonwealth were correct in what they asserted then Anne Frank would have been sent back to her attic on the grounds that she could live there safely, free from the attentions of the SS or anyone else looking for her.

These empirical findings are consistent with Halliday's findings in relation to Homeless Persons Units (HPUs) in the UK, where three housing authorities each noted that their experiences of judicial review had taught them the importance of articulating their decisions carefully and, somewhat artificially, to record the factors that they had 'considered' in the course of their decision making to proof against review.[24] This approach reflects a more widely documented process that Sunkin and Le Sueur have called 'bullet-proofing',[25] where government agencies use legal knowledge to immunise their decisions against potential judicial scrutiny. Such findings were certainly consistent with those individuals who expressed a repeated valuation of explicit legal identification here, where the ultimate goal for these individuals was not the substantive justice or outcome for the applicant but the application and articulation of legal doctrine. One participant, for example, expressed,

> The advice that I would give to anyone would be that you have to act without fear. If you make a decision that you are 100 percent comfortable with, then as far as I am concerned you have done the right thing. No matter what the outcome is, for me – if I felt comfortable that I made a lawful decision, then I was happy with that; no matter what the outcome was.[26]

Here, the participant, Anna Starkos, denies the importance of the outcome for the applicant; such considerations are not relevant where the decision maker applies the law to 'act without fear'. When presented with the same hypothetical fact scenario regarding the Hazara applicant from Jaghori, already discussed in relation to Frank Grey, she presented a radically different account of the important factors to consider. Where Grey was driven by concern for the substantive justice of the applicant – preoccupied with questions of how the decision maker can utilise his or her tacit knowledge to understand the situation for the applicant and come to a fair decision – Starkos was contrastingly concerned with reciting the *Refugee Convention* to come to a decision. When asked if a Hazara from Afghanistan who was claiming to have fled to Australia to escape the avengers of his father's warlord, Starkos replied,

> I guess the most obvious thing: is there a Convention ground here? This is the first thing that comes to my mind. Arguably there is at least one, which is imputed political opinion. Arguably there is at least one. It could be religion also; it could be race. So, the story, when you read it, sounds plausible to me; yes, perfectly plausible. So my initial reaction was that I am dealing with a plausible sequence of events and yes it is entirely plausible that this has happened.

The sentiment expressed here is similar to what Halliday finds, where his front-line officials in UK HPUs are involved in a process of 'information bingeing', where they collect information about applicants in rote, regardless of the applicant's circumstances and where there was no necessary connection among the information obtained, the demonstration of the 'factors' considered and the reason for the decision made.[27] Many of the interviewed RRT officials in this study engage in the specific process of 'law bingeing', perhaps a narrower iteration of what Halliday calls 'information bingeing', where law is recited and retrieved (without being contextually applied to the facts at hand in any sufficient kind of detail) to allegedly bolster the validity of one's decision. Multiple interviewees recited stand-alone legislative provisions at different points of the interview conversations: sections of the *Refugee Convention*, *Migration Act*, *Migration Regulations* and various case-law tests such as the 'reasonable person' doctrine, the 'safe third country principle' and the 'real chance test'. Such recitations were, unexceptionally, presented in contextual isolation from any factual scenario, such that their relevance to decision making was not communicated. In these utterances, individuals expressed a strong regard for explicit forms of knowledge, which is little more than stand-alone data or information. Such utterances failed to produce any real knowledge and certainly did not strive towards substantive justice for the applicant; these higher aims were contrastingly captured in moments when responsive legality drove decision making.

This compromise of substantive justice for law-related information bingeing is exemplified in one participant's reflections:

> That was something I had to get up to speed on: legal rhetoric . . . it was an evolving thing, you know, whether there is a real chance and what is being satisfied and not. I mean, those things are being defined and redefined all the time; every other month there was something new that came out of it and then everyone would have to learn the new thing, you know. And I found that was good; I think because it trained you to really think clearly about what you are trying to say instead of using coverall phrases. But at the same time it encouraged you to use coverall phrases, and if you found it difficult to plaster your decision with that stuff then you were struggling. So there was that, I wouldn't say it was 'cutting corners' but it was . . . it didn't make you really . . . it was tempting to kind of do that without actually getting to grips with the case sometimes.[28]

For participants displaying a strong regard for explicit legal knowledge – the law was a guard to hide behind to protect one's decision from jurisdictional error. The emphasis in these moments shifted from the consideration of substantive justice for the applicant onto the self-preservation of the decision maker. On the contrary, when individuals were driven by concerns for substantive justice they were not afraid to critique the law's capacity to produce the correct outcome, and they were concerned with contextualising the factual information of the case within the precise legal provision. Whilst those idealising and expressing explicit legal knowledge recite meaningless data, those intent on contextualising the plight of the applicant with regards to the broader legal and cultural framework construct meaningful knowledge in the pursuance of applicant welfare.

Here, a clear conceptual triad emerges, where the officials' idealisation of ***truth verification*** to produce contextual understandings of the applicant for the systemic goal of ***substantive justice*** requires and celebrates a kind of ***tacit knowledge valuation***. This triad was evident in the way that such individuals utilised metaphor and analogy in interview to express the importance of a contextual understanding of the applicant's situation – here, they simultaneously expressed their desire to get to the bottom of the factual scenario of the applicant using figures of speech in the form of analogies in an attempt to tacitly communicate this prioritisation of tacit values in interview. In such utterances, the interviewees expressed a clear appreciation for the importance of ***true understanding*** being imparted into the receiver, valuing actual knowledge transmittance (as opposed to superficial explicit knowledge) within the interview forum itself.

Exemplifying this pattern, one interviewee discussed the importance of obtaining a true understanding of the living situation of the applicant in simultaneous disregard for the importance of case law as an influence on decision making, metaphorically depicting the rule in a case as 'a handy cluster of considerations',[29] rather than 'informatively' regurgitating the rule itself. Recall Grey, discussed previously in this chapter, who, again expressing a strong regard for substantive justice for the applicant, a high regard for truth verification and a low identification with law, analogically asserts that

> [if there were a multi-member panel] It would be good to have at least one member of the multi-member panel who's got some knowledge of life outside Australia. I mean there are many people on the tribunal who are not diplomats and who have not lived in a third world country. And it really is very different. You can't imagine how different it is living in a third world country to living in Australia. Even in a relatively advanced third world country. And to understand the culture of other countries – but to really understand, not just read a book or understand the legal reasons – but to know the people, to have talked to them; to have been in their homes and sort of know the way that they think and live and what it's like. I was talking to a client yesterday from Iran. She has an uncle here who's giving her lots of advice, and she said 'the problem is he hasn't been back to Iran for thirty years; he doesn't know what it's like there'. And he's Iranian. Now how much more difficult is it for an Australian who's never been to Iran. See. And it is so important.[30]

Here, the interviewee is not talking about an applicant from the RRT at all; he is using the example of a conversation with an Iranian client (in his current position as a refugee barrister) to illuminate what he perceives to be the substantial injustice that can result from an inability to verify the truth and understand the real-world context of the applicant. In using the central analogical device of exemplification, the interviewee attempts to tacitly reach the interviewer to communicate his knowledge. Such analogical devices were commonly used as participants attempted to communicate their beliefs in the importance of verifying the truth, contextualising tacit understandings of the applicant and pursuing substantive justice simultaneously, where participants in these utterances provided large amounts of allegorical detail about former applicants to illustrate their concerns. Another participant similarly used allegory to critique the limitations of the legal regime in sceptical disregard for its capacity to achieve substantive justice, making comments such as the following:

> The courts are much more narrow in a way . . . what I'm trying to say is this. They give members too broad a brush to write sloppy decisions in some instances where they read them beneficially . . . that's my view of these Federal Court and Federal Circuit decisions because they don't know how the system really works from the inside.[31]

Here, the notion that court decisions give members too 'broad a brush' to write sloppy decisions metaphorically communicates a belief that the legal regime cannot understand the real working of the system absent tacit knowledge of how it operates from the inside.

Another excerpt summarises this recurrent use of analogy that communicates the low legal identification triad of prioritisation of *truth verification* to produce contextual understandings of the applicant for the systemic goal of substantive justice, both requiring and celebrating tacit knowledge valuation:

> I don't think so. I mean the sorts of things . . . if somebody's making a claim about, you know, something that's happened at their home or I don't know, let's say [applicants from] China . . . talk about the police coming round or the neighbourhood committee or how they couldn't do anything privately without, say, the neighbourhood committee knowing. Now if you have never been to China, which I haven't, and you are trying to picture what it's like, it's hard to assess people. They would say 'oh, well, we would have underground church services in their home so that they were secret and nobody ever knew about them', and you might think sometimes 'mmmm, is that really likely that you were able to do that; that you would have all these people arriving in your house and that nobody noticed?'. When you haven't been somewhere, you can't even really picture what it might be. And I always found that one of the biggest challenges.[32]

Another participant explained,

> It's hard to explain it because meeting someone from Afghanistan in one moment and the next person from Somalia and the next person from Mali or wherever they come from, that rich tapestry of human connection means that you were equipped to understand.[33]

All this is to elucidate the connection among truth verification, substantive justice and tacit knowledge valuation that accompanies the socially aware and purposive manipulation of the letter of the law. Whilst public officials engage in the regurgitation of stand-alone information in a futile quest for bureaucratic rationality, also compromising substantive justice goals in the process, these same individuals' analogical attempts to tacitly communicate the factual difficulties and truth-related ambiguities inherent in their decision making reflect an admirable regard for, and journey towards, broader justice-related system goals. If the plight of the applicant is not thoroughly investigated with an eye for optimal factual accuracy, the law-conscious information-binger will never be able to share the feed. To the contrary, processes and outcomes can be more equitably allocated when officials and organisations draw on a range of personal experiences to empathise with the applicants and citizens they serve.

Notes

1 Ralph Stair and George Reynolds, *Principles of Information Systems: A Managerial Approach* (International Thompson Publishing, 1998) 5.
2 Ibid 25.
3 Ibid.
4 Michelle Marinez, 'The Collective Power of Employee Knowledge' (1998) 43(2) *HR Magazine* 88–94.
5 See, for example, Denis Bonner, 'Knowledge: From Theory to Practice to Golden Opportunity' (2000) 134 *American Society for Training and Development?* 12–13; J Lee, 'Knowledge Management: The Intellectual Revolution' (2000) *IIE Solutions* 102; Eric Smith, 'The Role of Tacit Knowledge and Explicit Knowledge in the Workplace' (2001) 5(4) *Journal of Knowledge Management* 311–21; Laurie Wah, 'Making Knowledge Stick' (1999) *Management Review* 24–9.
6 Geoff Walshman, 'Knowledge Management: The Benefits and Limitations of Computer Systems' (2001) 19(6) *European Management Journal* 599–608.
7 Merle Jacob and Golaleh Ebrahimpur, 'Experience vs. Expertise: The Role of Implicit Understandings of Knowledge in Determining the Nature of Knowledge Transfer in Two Companies' (2001) 2(1) *Journal of Intellectual Capital* 74–8.
8 Bruno Latour, *Science in Action: How to Follow Scientists and Engineers Through Society* (Open University Press, 1987) 248.
9 Rodney McAdam and Simon McCreedy, 'The Emerging Trend of Knowledge Management Within Organisations: A Critical Assessment of Both Theory and Practice' (1998) Paper presented at 1998 Annual Conference of the British Academy of Management, University of Nottingham.
10 Richard Daft and Robert Lengel, 'Information Richness: A New Approach to Managerial Behaviour and Organisational Design' in B Staw and L Cummings (eds), *Research in Organisational Behviour* (JAI Press, 1984) vol 6, 139.
11 Refer to Chapter 1 for a discussion.
12 Jerry Mashaw, *Bureaucratic Justice: Managing Social Security Disability Claims* (Yale University Press, 1983).
13 Ibid 52.
14 Ibid 51.
15 Interview with [Anonymous Participant B], (semi-structured interview) (28 November 2013).
16 Interview with [Anonymous Participant J], (semi-structured interview) (16 December 2013).
17 Interview with [Anonymous Participant Y], (semi-structured interview) (28 January 2014).
18 Interview with [Anonymous Participant K], (semi-structured interview) (16 December 2013).

19 Interview with [Anonymous Participant W], (semi-structured interview) (22 January 2014).
20 Patricia Ewick and Susan Silbey, *The Common Place of Law* (The University of Chicago Press, 1998) 196.
21 Ibid 196.
22 Interview with [Anonymous Participant K], (semi-structured interview) (18 December 2013).
23 Interview with [Anonymous Participant G], (semi-structured interview) (11 December 2013).
24 Simon Halliday, *Judicial Review and Compliance with Administrative Law* (Hart Publishing, 2004) 64.
25 Maurice Sunkin and Andrew Le Sueur, 'Conceptual Issues in Researching the Impact of Judicial Review on Government Bureaucracies' in Marc Hertogh and Simon Halliday (eds), *Judicial Review and Bureaucratic Impact* (Cambridge University Press, 2004).
26 Interview with [Anonymous Participant C], (semi-structured interview) (3 December 2013).
27 Halliday, above n 50, 64.
28 Interview with [Anonymous Participant H], (semi-structured interview) (11 December 2013).
29 Interview with [Anonymous Participant A], (semi-structured interview) (8 November 2013).
30 Interview with [Anonymous Participant G], (semi-structured interview) (11 December 2013).
31 Interview with [Anonymous Participant N], (semi-structured interview) (23 December 2013).
32 JT interview at 2.
33 Interview with [Anonymous Participant Y], (semi-structured interview) (28 January 2014).

Reference list

Articles/books/reports

Bonner, Denis, 'Knowledge: From Theory to Practice to Golden Opportunity' (2000) 134 *American Society for Training and Development?* 12

Hertogh, Marc and Simon Halliday, *Judicial Review and Bureaucratic Impact* (Cambridge University Press, 2004)

Jacob, Merle and Golaleh Ebrahimpur, 'Experience vs. Expertise: The Role of Implicit Understandings of Knowledge in Determining the Nature of Knowledge Transfer in Two Companies' (2001) 2(1) *Journal of Intellectual Capital* 74

Latour, Bruno, *Science in Action: How to Follow Scientists and Engineers Through Society* (Open University Press, 1987)

Lee, James, 'Knowledge Management: The Intellectual Revolution' (2000) *IIE Solutions* 102

Marinez, Michelle, 'The Collective Power of Employee Knowledge' (1998) 43(2) *HR Magazine* 88

Mashaw, Jerry, *Bureaucratic Justice: Managing Social Security Disability Claims* (Yale University Press, 1983)

McAdam, Rodney and Simon McCreedy, 'The Emerging Trend of Knowledge Management Within Organisations: A Critical Assessment of Both Theory and Practice'

(1998) Paper presented at 1998 Annual Conference of the British Academy of Management, University of Nottingham, Nottingham

Smith, Elizabeth, 'The Role of Tacit Knowledge and Explicit Knowledge in the Workplace' (2001) 5(4) *Journal of Knowledge Management* 311–21

Stair, Ralph and George Reynolds, *Principles of Information Systems: A Managerial Approach* (International Thompson Publishing, 1998)

Staw, B and L Cummings, *Research in Organisational Behaviour* (JAI Press, 1984)

Wah, Laurie, 'Making Knowledge Stick' (1999) *Management Review* 24

Walshman, Geoff, 'Knowledge Management: The Benefits and Limitations of Computer Systems' (2001) 19(6) *European Management Journal* 599

Other

Interview with [Anonymous Participant A], (semi-structured interview) (8 November 2013)

Interview with [Anonymous Participant B], (semi-structured interview) (28 November 2013)

Interview with [Anonymous Participant C], (semi-structured interview) (3 December 2013)

Interview with [Anonymous Participant G], (semi-structured interview) (11 December 2013)

Interview with [Anonymous Participant H], (semi-structured interview) (11 December 2013)

Interview with [Anonymous Participant J], (semi-structured interview) (16 December 2013)

Interview with [Anonymous Participant N], (semi-structured interview) (23 December 2013)

Interview with [Anonymous Participant Y], (semi-structured interview) (28 January 2014)

6 Protecting welfare through the rule of law

Introduction

This chapter explores the underlying mode of responsive legality: protecting applicant welfare through applying the rule of law. When justifying their decisions according to this type, public officials are genuinely and empathetically concerned with the well-being of the applicant and believe that this welfare will be achieved, in part, at least, through rule-of-law compliance. Of course, for responsive legality to be present, decision makers must also be driven by valuations of responsiveness, joint procedural and substantive justice concerns and the application of cognitive processes of truth verification and information processing. In a way, this 'mode' of protecting welfare through the rule of law might therefore be thought of as an amalgamation of the other features of the type (where concepts of protecting welfare through law are already essentially covered in exploring the other component features of the type in their emphasis on responsiveness and procedural justice). As such, though conscious of the overlaps with the other features of the type as presented in the previous chapters, this chapter adds nuance to understandings of this relationship through specifically considering how variations in attitudes towards law can alter the normative strength of officials' administrative justice positions. In so doing, it applies a socio-legal legal consciousness analysis to consider how officials' attitudes towards law parallel their variations in constructions of administrative justice. In this endeavour, it argues that officials who strategically use the law to achieve positive outcomes for applicants – when also demonstrating the other component features of responsive legality – come markedly further in achieving positive visions of administrative justice than in moments when they position themselves 'against the law' or – acting *only* in their own self-interest – 'with the law' – tainting the administration in these moments with the negative features of self-serving rule-of-law compliance.

Public officials' normative justificatory logistics and the legal consciousness enquiry

Legal consciousness studies

Legal consciousness: development and rationales

In order to illustrate the important role that purposive and welfare-oriented rule-of-law compliance plays in the preferred responsive-legality type, and the reasons why it is presented as preferable, this section provides a brief background to the legal consciousness literature – drawn on to illuminate the complex relationships between officials' legal attitudes and broader normative positions.

By way of background, the history, the development and the growth of legal consciousness studies, which have been prominent within socio-legal studies since at least the 1980s, have been summarised numerous times.[1] Despite varying descriptions of their precise starting date[2] and their overall value,[3] these summaries unite in affirming that legal consciousness studies have played a central role within socio-legal studies over at least the last 30 years.[4] Whilst legal consciousness studies were originally, and are predominantly, US-based, the theoretical frame became increasingly popular in European socio-legal research in the early 2000s.

Susan Silbey recounts that legal consciousness as a theoretical frame and subject of empirical enquiry developed within law and society research in the 1980s and 1990s to explore issues of legal hegemony, focusing on the question of why people acquiesce to a legal system that systematically produces inequality despite its promises of equal treatment. Silbey explains that such studies found, repeatedly, a troubling gap between law on the books and law in action – a division that lies at the heart of law and society research more broadly. Whether in historical studies of litigation, studies of the legal profession, studies of policing, histories of how legal doctrines or offices developed, judicial biographies and studies of court cultures, studies of business regulation or studies of crime control, broader law and society research until the 1970s and 1980s had confirmed that organisational structures, social institutions and local cultures intricately shaped the uses and impacts of law. Out of this finding emerged the narrower question at the heart of legal consciousness research of how 'we the people'[5] might be contributing to the law's ineffectiveness and its systemic production of inequality. Thus, in the 1980s, the question of the way that law is experienced and understood by ordinary citizens – the question underpinning legal consciousness research – became a central focus for many law and society scholars. As David Engel outlines, the very earliest legal consciousness studies 'contained an initial exploration of positively conceived social facts or events [which] began to collapse back into subjectivity, meaning and cognition'.[6]

Similar concerns about the way social facts and events collapse into subjectivity, meaning and cognition motivate this present study into the normative logics (including legal attitudes) of public officials. Now that we know much about what individual citizens think about law (to the extent that Silbey argues that studies of the legal consciousness of ordinary citizens have been so similar and numerous that researchers are failing to unearth new findings), this framework can be productively applied to the new enquiry into the subjective and cognitive meaning making of government officials to reveal the other part of the story regarding citizens' subjugation: the role of those making the decisions in the production of citizen outcomes. Whilst Silbey has recently critiqued the future of the enterprise on the basis that legal consciousness studies are generally unlikely to discern generalisable truths in a fragmented postmodern age or achieve much more than satisfy the researcher's empiricist desires to 'reach out and touch',[7] she has left open the possibility that there is more to be done when it comes to understanding legal consciousness in relation to modern institutional settings such as that of government. For Silbey,

> [t]he most promising work seems to look at the middle level between citizen and the transcendental rule of law: the ground of institutional practices. In institutions cultural meaning, social inequality, and legal consciousness are forged. In institutions law both promises and fails to live up to its promises. One place to begin is the cultural industries where legal consciousness is most explicitly constructed. To describe the mechanisms by which legal schema are propagated, circulated, and received, we need institutional approaches that describe simultaneously the full range of social construction.[8]

Whether or not Sibley's broader critique of legal consciousness is accepted, the importance of legal consciousness in government studies – as with all socio-legal law in the books and law in action gap studies – can be revealed, as Marc Hertogh outlines, through the analogy of a person walking onto the street and meeting cold weather and wind chill.[9] Whilst the thermometer may only read –2 degrees Celsius, the wind may be blowing at 45 kilometres per hour so that the wind-chill factor causes it to feel like it is –10 degrees Celsius. For a true understanding of local weather conditions and its *effects*, one should take into account the objective and subjective elements. The same of course holds true for understanding how law intersects with the normative logics of public officials to motivate administrative action. Reading decisions, or statutes, or policy documents, or training manuals will only tell us so much; for the rest of the picture, we must examine, analytically and empirically, the public officials and organisations themselves to better understand how law works and responds with applicant's needs in public administration. The legal consciousness framework therefore provides a helpful set of tools for thinking about how officials embrace, or at times subvert, the rule of law to better understand the role of law as a component feature of the normative logic justifying administrative action.

This present discussion of the role that decision makers' responses to law play in contributing to their normative justice orientations also emulates the theoretical and methodological leanings of the traditional citizen-based legal consciousness enquiry. Whilst much socio-legal research has emphasised law's instrumental role within society – considering the way that law acts on society from an external position – legal consciousness studies take the constitutive question of how law shapes actors' understandings of social relations and vice versa, as its core concern. Whilst instrumental and constitutive conceptions of law and society are not to be viewed as mutually exclusive, an enquiry that is predominantly constitutive in focus may provide a more nuanced account of law in action, which an instrumental view alone cannot achieve.

This study's discussion of the public administrators' legal attitudes and constitutive normative justice orientations also emulates the traditional methodology of legal consciousness studies in its empirical dimensions. Indeed, for legal consciousness researchers, the enterprise has traditionally been importantly empirical.

Halliday and Morgan query, '[H]ow can we theorise about law's hegemonic power until we find out exactly what society thinks, feels and does about law?'[10] The distinction between law on the books and law in action in terms of individual citizens reactions to law cannot be ascertained through normative theorisation itself, which would leave the 'action' part of the equation blank. Empirical enquiry therefore becomes a necessary starting point for later normative legal consciousness theory building.

Legal consciousness: popular conceptualisations

The present study also draws on a number of popular conceptualisations of what is meant by legal consciousness. Since legal consciousness studies began, varying aspects of legal consciousness have been emphasised by different researchers. Broadly speaking, popular definitions of legal consciousness have morphed over time, from early legal consciousness studies that focused on quantifying levels of public knowledge towards law in the 1970s, to more theoretically sophisticated investigations into the complex presence of law in society in the 1990s. Whilst the former studies tended to use large-scale quantitative survey data to examine levels of awareness about law and to compare such data to the content of legal provisions, the latter tended to qualitatively explore the intersectionality of law and social life in legal culture. This has led more recent legal consciousness researchers to explore 'images of law and legal institutions that people carry around in their heads and occasionally act upon'.[11] They are less concerned with 'testing' or 'measuring' compliance with law and more concerned with building deeper understandings of how law itself becomes an overarching concept constituted by particular aspects of social practice.

The theory in this book adopts the latter contemporary approach to studying legal consciousness, considering the qualitative dimensions of the legal consciousness of public officials to explore the images of law and legal institutions that these officials 'carry around in their heads'.[12] This approach is particularly motivated by the legal consciousness literature, which has, since the 1990s, advocated this more nuanced qualitative approach.

Though its application to the theory in this book has changed through its many research lives, the legal consciousness framework has remained of enduring value in thinking about the normative logics motivating public administrators' conceptions of administrative justice, as stark synergies between the officials' attitudes towards law and justice revealed themselves in the interdisciplinary literature and empirical enquiry. The framework revealed clear parallels between how the participants thought about law and the broader bases on which they justified their decisions – assisting in understanding the relationship between rule-of-law compliance and the officials' normative-justice orientations.

The central framework that helped to illuminate these relationships and reveal more about the responsive-legality type was Patricia Ewick and Susan Silbey's investigation into the legal consciousness of the everyday lives of ordinary American citizens,[13] which is the iconic and foundational study within the field. Ewick and Silbey's study has paved the way for how researchers define notions of legal consciousness and often provided the foundation for constructing further redefinitions – or, at times, departures. Through informal interview conversations with 430 New Jersey residents, they found that individuals are positioned either 'before the law', 'with the law' or 'against the law', noting that the typology is not meant to function as a confined way of understanding individuals across all points in time but as a set of prototypes to be drawn on in different ways at different times.

They posit that because social life is shifting and law goes through complex iterations of being invoked, not invoked, ignored and resisted, it is assigned a malleable role in people's everyday lives that is socially contingent and changing. Thus, according to Ewick and Silbey and as seen in the studies of many legal consciousness researchers after them, legal consciousness is best studied in terms of abstracted categories that may be mostly, but not necessarily unexceptionally, observable in a particular context. The bulk of legal consciousness research therefore defines legal consciousness broadly – investigating how and what individuals think about law – to extract further ideal types associated with varying levels of consciousness in order to stress certain elements common to most cases of the given phenomena.

Within this breadth of definition, contemporary scholars of legal consciousness are intent on uncovering not just how and by whom the law is used and understood but also a better understanding about how individuals' subconscious ideas about law can form part of their legal attitudes, experiences and understandings. Sally Engle Merry begins with a definition of legal consciousness as 'the ways people understand and use law'[14] in her study of working-class American interactions with the justice system in two New England towns. She goes on to elaborate that consciousness refers not only to deliberate and intentional action but also to the quotidian habitual action and practice 'embedded in the practical constitution of everyday life'.[15] Likewise, Laura Beth Nielson, in her study of the attitudes of ordinary citizens towards law and street harassment, emphasises that the study of legal consciousness 'not only explores how people think about law (consciousness about law) but also the ways in which largely *un*conscious ideas about the law can affect the decisions that they make'.[16]

The framework of responsive legality presented in this book, and the particular focus on the officials' attitudes towards law and how they affect their normative justice orientations in this chapter, draws on these rich approaches. It notes, as the tradition attests, that legal consciousness may involve considerations of people's understandings and awareness of the law, as well as their subconscious attitudes towards the law and its importance. It retains the belief that understandings of what legal consciousness involves might therefore continue to be built empirically, as observations of the operation or non-operation of law in the social world continue to provide ideal types for understanding iterations of legal consciousness – feeding back into foundational understandings of how law is subjectively perceived and applied.

This study also proceeds cognisant of Halliday and Morgan's assertion that because legal consciousness studies focus on the ordinary, quotidian and invisible aspects of law in social life, they can reach beneath the surface to unearth a wealth of information about how law, in practice, shapes multiple dimensions of society that go beyond the scope and subject matter of doctrinal legal research as well as socio-legal research that does not take constitutive questions of human consciousness at its core. The agenda of legal consciousness research is to unearth deeper understandings of pervasive human commonalities, and in doing so, attempt to reach to the heart of how law is understood, constructed, manipulated and subverted in human minds and hands. As Hertogh outlines, without studying the wind-chill factor, we cannot understand the true weather conditions, and without studying legal consciousness, we cannot understand the true conditions and operationalisation of law. Likewise, it is asserted here that without studying the varying legal attitudes of administrative officials, we cannot fully contemplate their normative justice orientations. This is indeed acknowledged in Adler's legal type of administrative justice, which sees legality as the cornerstone of good administration. Building further nuance into this type, it is asserted here that the application of the legal consciousness framework to the normative justice project can tell us much about how variations in officials' attitudes towards law parallel the normative logics that they draw on to justify their decisions, adding further nuance to these models and, as shall be demonstrated, providing a further foundation for their normative evaluation.

The remainder of this chapter revisits empirical portions of the study presented in previous chapters, keeping with the favoured legal consciousness approach, for the purposes of teasing out the way variations in rule-of-law valuation correspond with the participants' legitimating values, equality orientation and cognitive techniques. In this, it revisits the previously presented studies from a slightly different perspective – emphasising the narrower question of the role that the officials' attitudes towards law play in altering the normative-justice orientations they mobilise to justify their decisions. It is hoped that this is not a repetitive rehash of empirical material for the reader but, rather, that this repetition might consolidate the varying features of the officials' normative-justice orientations and culminate in a more nuanced illustration of the positive features of responsive legality for public administration.

Stories of law and justice

'Against the law'

Bureaucratic legal consciousness and conceptions of substantive justice

At many points, participant officials positioned themselves 'against the law'; they were cynical of its ability to achieve good governance and substantive justice for applicants. In these moments, officials could be clearly likened to Ewick and Silbey's participant citizens who in this vision of law construed legality as something to be avoided. On this view of legality, when it comes to general citizens, law is viewed as specifically limited in that it is unable to cope with the ordinary troubles that characterise daily life. It is argued here that these 'against-the-law' attitudes commonly correspond with admirable valuations of substantive justice but that a lack of concern for procedural consistency inherent in this type can invite the perils of repressive governance that Nonet and Selznick warn against.

Whilst this argument is made as a basic general analytical observation regarding the intuitive, logical connections between these ways of thinking, these connections are illustrated with reference to the empirical interview material below. As shall be explored, at many moments decision makers aligned with Ewick and Silbey's 'against-the-law' image of legality; they uniformly denied the centrality of legal rules, regulations or procedures to conducting good RRT decision making and instead alleged that good decision making commonly required the perception of the real-world truth of the applicant's situation as verified through external fact checking. Justice, in these moments, required more than what could be embodied in procedure alone. Justice, far from consistency, required the individualised delivery of fair outcomes.

Georgia Boulos[17] was one participant recurrently positioned 'against the law' and reflecting a substantive justice orientation. She discussed the superficiality of the law and the law's inability to answer the deep and complex issues required for good decision making on the RRT. As an immigrant to Australia herself, Boulos had experienced difficulties of relocation and stigmatisation that she believed were crucial cultural components to understanding applicants in migration contexts. She reflected on her time working with migrant women's collective movements in Australia in the 1970s and 1980s and then moving on to conduct migrant-related research for a number of commissions and councils after having completed her university degree in the humanities. Boulos was at many points sceptical of the role of law in providing a mechanism for good decision making, claiming that the legally trained staff often performed what she thought was 'mindless research', whereas she preferred a 'holistic approach'. She discussed how she had done a range of work for the Premier of an Australian state and had also worked extensively in ethnic affairs. She discussed how she transposed a number of these experiences and the knowledge she had gained from this work into her RRT decision making to enrich her decision making. She described, for example, a system she introduced into her own office when she worked in state government where she transformed a file number system into one arranged by topics. Boulos discussed that she applied this approach to the RRT, introducing a system where individual decision makers would specialise in deciding claims for applicants in specific countries of origin, as this provided a more thorough investigation into the depth of the applicant's claim.

Recurrent in Boulos's narrative was a discussion of the important justice goals driving good decision making that were not achieved through a consideration of the law alone. When asked whether she had observed if legally and non-legally trained members made similar decisions or followed similar decision-making processes, Boulos disregarded the question of law and legal training, claiming instead,

> Look, I consistently aimed for social justice. Justice is very important. And I mean I was also involved in the women's movement and the migrant ethnic affairs movement, and justice and fairness was obviously something that was strong in me.

For Boulos, this social justice experience was paramount in achieving substantive justice for the applicant, and it made her more sensitive to the deep and complex issues inherent in RRT decision making that a consideration of the law alone could not. Justice was about more than process for Boulos. It was not about having consistent approaches to decision making between individuals. To the contrary, Boulos reflected that individuals had very different approaches to decision making – including her and her husband, who was a lawyer, and she believed that that difference was okay. Rather than aiming towards consistency, the production of justice required utilising one's own personal experience to discern the intricacies of the specific claim.

Boulos told the story of a case where the applicant was Guatemalan and had travelled to Argentina and then to Chile, had been refused refugee status in Chile and then travelled to Australia. She recounted, '[T]he guy seemed to me really sophisticated and his English was very good. He had an accent, but [his English] was very, very good. And he was too sophisticated for the claims he was making'. She went on to say that because she had lived in South America, she knew when a South American person was telling the truth. She recounted that the applicant claimed that part of his job in Guatemala was ice fishing, but Boulos was proud to declare, 'Well, let me tell you there ain't any ice fishing in Guatemala', and went on to explain, 'And I didn't even have to think about it. He just knocked himself out. See, it's not something that I could overlook because it is just so second nature to my basic knowledge'. Boulos reiterated the importance of individualised substantive justice through fair outcomes for applicants, claiming, 'I feel that you really need to address yourself to the particulars. It's not a simple method kind of approach'.

For Boulos, the law was superficial in dealing with the complex human problems that presented themselves in a refugee claim. Law was not necessarily a deterrent away from good decision making, but it certainly was not the answer. It could not produce substantive justice in the form of an outcome that comprehends the truth of the applicant's story to protect them from persecution. In these narratives, the law provided part of the framework for good decision making at most but was a superficial device for achieving true substantive justice to the extent that it did not account for many of the complexities only learnt through personal life experience.

Like Boulos, David Dominish[18] also often sat 'against the law'. He recurrently presented an image of law as constraining: as a limited tool for achieving fair outcomes for applicants. Dominish had grown up in Sri Lanka, studied Buddhism and Asian Studies at university in Sydney and worked as a member of parliament for the Australian Liberal Party for many years. He had a deep interest in foreign affairs and had worked as High Commissioner for the United Nations, including in South Africa under Mandela. Whilst at times Dominish was highly legalistic – revering law for its difficulty, its rationality, its structure and its certainty – at other times, when personal experience was the ideal driving his reflections, the law was limited in its ability to deliver fair outcomes; it was a constraining body of rules that failed to connect with applicants in the way that personal experience facilitated. For Dominish, discussing his experience with the United Nations and in politics, 'you need something more than the law; you need people with judgement and hopefully with some experience'. Whilst he presented a nuanced account of the strengths and weaknesses of law, alleging that there are both positive and negative aspects of coming from a legal background as a decision maker, the limitations of the law derived from its separateness from the virtues instilled through personal experience. He reflected,

> I think there are both strengths and weaknesses if you come from a different non-legal background. Because you bring a much broader life experience to the role . . . that's a very important aspect, because you have to be able to understand that there is life outside of a small confinement of words or the legal area. So there is a strength in that: that you can perhaps suss out or you can tease out the nuances of what a person has tried to tell you, because many of these people are extremely frightened of anything to do with the law or anything that gives a sense of authority.

For Dominish, having lived and worked in many Asian and African countries and having experienced much of life outside Australia and outside the law, a good decision maker needed 'to be able to understand that there is life outside of a small confinement of words or the legal area'. Dominish emphasised in these moments that to connect with applicants in hearing one needed to be able to use everyday language rather than being confined to using legal terminology, which would fail to reach lay applicants.

Dominish reflected on the limitations of the law in achieving fair outcomes for individuals, commenting that following precedent would 'lead you in any situation really to find in favour of an applicant on review'. He went on to reflect, 'I mean, if you are of that mindset you have plenty of excuses to do that using precedent', construing the law as something that can be manipulated to give the illusion of fairness at the expense of real justice. In this conjoint vision of administrative justice and 'against-the-law' images of legality, Dominish describes the administrative justice system as 'a Rolls-Royce system on square wheels'. For Dominish, this is a system that is 'extremely expensive with a beautiful legal paraphernalia to go through but a pretty considerable lack of common sense in terms of how you actually handle the case'. In this, he reiterated that 'being a lawyer definitely did not give you a gold card to securing good outcomes' and that 'frankly, you have to have a high level of common sense'. For Dominish, the law was something that people could hide behind, but it would not lead to the correct decision being made

> because at the end of the day . . . if you just want to hide behind the law, you could pass 100 per cent of them if you wanted to. You could, no doubt. So you need something more than the law; you need people with judgement and hopefully some experience.

Like Dominish, Justine Anderson[19] also expressed a nuanced account of law as limited in achieving the substantive justice that required the application of a range of broader normative values. In these moments, Anderson expressed that the law was constraining at points where it did not adopt the values better taught through personal experience and was only perceived as enabling when alternate values of rationality, information processing and intelligence were embraced. Anderson had worked in family law for many years before beginning on the tribunal and explained that she came on the position at the RRT 'by chance' when a friend of hers saw the advertisement in the paper and recommended that she apply. She recounted the lengthy time it would take to write a decision, the various structural and administrative changes that the tribunal had undergone over the years and the onerous requirements to give notice to applicants before affirming their case. But even within these relatively dispassionate and mechanical accounts, Anderson's attitudes towards law appeared to oscillate in tandem with a broader moral framework, which idealised the non-legal 'human' or emotional virtues derived from personal experience, on one hand, and the rationality embodied in the law, on the other. In a moment of cynicism towards the law, Anderson offered,

> There is a range of elements to fair decision making that is not just about how to apply the law. In the narrow sense, applying the law is all about being a fair decision maker, so many non-legal members were very, very good members because they weren't constrained by technical legal aspects but they were just fair, decent human beings with some life experience who were able to effectively interact with the claimant and hear them fairly and come to a reasonable decision about what the claims were.

In this image of legality, law was a constraining force, limited by its technicalities and unable to produce the outcomes that were contrastingly produced by 'fair, decent human beings with some life experience'. In these moments, there was something inhumane about the letter of the law. There was a rigidity constraining it from connecting with applicants to achieve broader goals of substantively fair outcomes.

Daisy Hardgraves's[20] Latvian mother and Lithuanian father had migrated to Australia after having met in Germany in the 1940s. Both had previously fled the USSR. When asked why she took up the position on the tribunal, Hardgraves explained that she felt an affinity to the work because of the fact that her parents were displaced persons. Hardgraves had begun a law degree before starting on the tribunal and had almost completed it by the time she took up the position. However, for Hardgraves, there was a broad range of factors that shaped good RRT decisions, and the law was low amongst these.

Hardgraves expressed that law played a minimal role in shaping her decision making and that the changing situation in the applicant's country of feared persecution made the primary goal of fact-checking a very difficult one, rendering the application of the law essentially irrelevant to producing a substantively fair outcome. When asked whether knowledge of the law shaped her approach as a decision maker, she responded,

> No, no I don't think so. When I started on the RRT I had almost finished my law degree and frankly, I think that the law I did didn't really add to my knowledge of what I needed to know.

When asked if she could remember a difficult case that she had worked on, Hardgraves responded,

> Yeah, there was one that I can think of as one of the last ones that I did; it was a[n] Uyghur case from China, with the Uyghurs up in the Northern/Mongolian border where there is still unrest these days with the Han Chinese repopulating that area. And I remember a number of Sri Lankan cases being particularly difficult, because while I was on the tribunal the situation kept changing in terms of how dangerous it might be for someone in Colombo or if someone could relocate from Jatvah to, you know, somewhere else. So the Sri Lanka cases were always difficult . . . they were typically difficult because of the changing political situation.

In expressing a desire to externally verify truth claims, Hardgraves expressed a core challenge associated with RRT decision making in terms of the difficulty of assessing the truth of the applicant's situation. For Hardgraves, truth attainment was a practical possibility, despite being difficult, and it functioned as a primary goal of good RRT decision making. This was again expressed by Hardgraves when she was explicitly asked what the most important decision-making skills were. She gave the example of a Chinese applicant who had come before her who said that he was a persecuted Falun Gong leader in China and was claiming refugee status on that basis. Hardgraves recounted how the applicant entered the hearing in a very 'new looking' yellow T-shirt and had the Falun Gong book in his hands. Hardgraves recounted that when she saw that the book was new looking and that only the first few pages were worn she became 'suspicious that he might have been exaggerating his role'. In questioning the applicant at length to verify his status as a Falun Gong practitioner, Hardgraves recognised the limitations of the legal regime to solve the problem and the importance of substantive justice in terms of ensuring fair outcomes for applicants.

You will recall Frank Grey, who had no formal qualifications in law but prided himself in his background as 'if anything, a historian and an economist', and consistently reflected on the role that personal work and travel experience had played in providing a level of depth to decision making that the superficial letter of the law was unable to embody. Where Grey idealised personal experience and produced corresponding 'against-the-law' images of law's superficiality, in these same moments he often also idealised truth verification, discussing that the law was largely unhelpful and irrelevant.

Similarly, Carla Abdi[21] was sceptical of the ability of the law to produce the requisite substantive justice required in good decision making, presenting an image of the law as 'frightening' for 'applicants who have often waited a long time to get to the tribunal'. Abdi did not have a background in law but for many years before beginning on the tribunal had been a member of an Australian Parliament and on retiring from the tribunal became the CEO of a large and prominent Australian company. Whilst Abdi had filled a number of high-profile roles in both the private and the public sectors, she spoke about her role on the tribunal as the most 'intimidating' work she had undertaken because of the immense effects the decision maker has on applicants' lives. She reflected that determining issues of truthfulness was a difficult and intimidating task that did not always have a clear template to follow and that individuals' lives would importantly turn on what the decision maker perceived the factual truth to be.

For Abdi, the law did not provide a solution to the difficult task of distinguishing the applicants' truth from their lies. It was unable to answer the difficult question of when an applicant really was a refugee, and it could not guide the decision maker to make a correct decision on the facts. For Abdi,

> the business visas are in my view quite narrow as opposed to refugee cases where you really have to often make a difficult judgment about the person's integrity and whether or not you believe what they are telling you. They are nearly always afraid of the outcome, and the law won't help you with that.

Here, Abdi reflected on the difficulty of RRT decision making, construing it as frightening and alienating to the applicant who is 'nearly always afraid of the outcome'. She reflected that the law could not assist in producing the correct decision, or the decision that is normatively admirable or justified. This, for Abdi, can only come through the ability to distinguish the truth from the lies: to discern the 'deserving ones' from the 'queue jumpers'.

Dominish and Abdi presented common images of law as 'frightening', positioning themselves 'against the law' in that they were critical of its ability to produce substantive justice for the applicant and, in Dominish's case, its tendency instead to subdue the applicant into a sense of fear and intimidation. In these moments, both Dominish and Abdi idealised the ability to distinguish the truth from the lies, presenting images of law as 'frightening', commonly driven by an underlying valuation of truth verification associated with a clear regard for fair outcomes for the applicant.

'Before the law'

Bureaucratic legal consciousness and conceptions of procedural justice

This section continues the empirical examination of bureaucratic legal consciousness and administrative justice valuation. Within these narratives, justice goals were framed not in terms of fairness of outcomes but in terms of consistency of treatment – where what was seen as the goal of good decision making in these moments was that everyone was treated the same through the application of legal principle, without preference or bias.

At the same time, visions of justice in terms of consistent treatment for applicants were eroded in this narrative, as participants also discussed the importance of law as a 'shield' to protect their decisions from jurisdictional error. An overwhelming majority of the officials interviewed discussed the way that law was utilised defensively and self-protectively in their judgements to give the impression of having followed the correct procedure (i.e. having considered and applied the law) but that there were multiple aspects of the law that could be drawn on at various points in time such that the application of an allegedly 'consistent' body of principles was ultimately arbitrary and subjective in scope. It was often drawn upon to give the impression of consistency, when, in fact, this was commonly far from the reality. In these narratives, the law was a shield to protect the officials' decisions from jurisdictional error under the guise of procedural fairness.

Ewick and Silbey recount that their citizen participants positioned 'before the law' envisage and enact the law as if it is separate from ordinary social life. In this form of consciousness, the law is 'described as a formally ordered, rational and hierarchical system of known rules and procedures'.[22] Likewise, the officials studied here shared at many moments Ewick and Silbey's citizens' reverence for the 'rational' law, at these times telling stories of the law's 'awesome grandeur, something that transcends by its history and processes the persons and conflicts of the moment'.

Depicting this image of law as difficult was George Wilson,[23] who was a judge of nearly two decades. Wilson had extensive knowledge of the law and a nuanced attitude towards its helpfulness in RRT decision making. However, where in some moments – moments where experience and substantive justice for applicants were idealised – the law was an artificial tool that was somewhat sloppily copied and pasted into official reasons to bolster the alleged reliability of the decision, in other moments it was a great intellectual challenge and the proper basis of consistent, and therefore procedurally fair, RRT decision making. Being intelligent and being able to process large amounts of information were in these moments perceived as connected values that drove this image of law as difficult.

When asked what skills a good decision maker possessed, Wilson responded, 'Well, they understood how to write a decision. They understood what the law was . . . the basis of the decision making. They understood how you would test the information; what questions would seem sensible to ask someone'.

Wilson was careful to reiterate that there were no easy solutions to the difficult task of RRT decision making and no quick fixes or easy answers for bringing decision makers up to speed with the difficult law:

> I mean, I don't know what best way of assessing them is. I don't know what the best way is. I mean, one best way would be to give them all a lawyer; not an immigration agent but a proper lawyer who knew what they were doing and then get them to say 'blah blah blah'.

Whilst there was not necessarily one clear answer to ensuring good decision making, the provision of a lawyer – not a migration agent who was not thoroughly trained in law – was the most promising solution. For Wilson, proper lawyers 'knew what they were doing' and could negotiate the complexities of the legal regime and sift through the relevant information to come to a correct decision.

In response to a question about whether or not decision makers who were 'proper lawyers', as he put it, could get a sense of whether the applicant was telling the truth, Wilson replied,

> Oh, I wouldn't say that. I wouldn't say that I can tell whether they are telling the truth. But the story just seems a bit more consistent, and so you'd get an idea that at least hangs together; whether it is the truth is another question. But oh no, I would never. That's what people used to say when they said that you can always tell, I said 'no you can't'. That's what I used to say. I mean, I had done it for 25 years. I mean, in the end you say that you believe them or you don't believe them, but particularly refugees, it is very, very difficult. You'd have to go through the whole process: Where did you come from? What's your date of birth? And all that.

In these moments Wilson reflected 'before-the-law' images of legality and recurrent regard for information processing in the pursuit of procedural justice. He expressed that it is important that the decision maker be a 'proper lawyer' and that he or she 'know[s] the law', rather than discern the truth, which is an impossible task without full knowledge of the facts and the ability to verify external information. For Wilson, whilst the internal consistency of the applicant's story could be logically monitored, this would not necessarily produce an answer that aligned with an external reality, though it could deliver a sense of natural justice to the applicant. Whether the outcome for the applicant is 'correct' in these moments is not the point; the best version of justice that could be done is the one that treats all applicants the same through the difficult application of a consistent body of legal principles.

This narrative of law as difficult, and its correspondence with broader idealisations of intellect for the attainment of procedural justice, is also reflected by Sue Poukchanski,[24] who recurrently discussed the centrality of the difficult legal regime to good RRT decision making. Poukchanski had worked as an academic, having completed her PhD in the 1980s in New South Wales and commenced a postdoctoral research position in the UK before working for government departments in a research capacity for a number of years after that. Poukchanski was also a refugee herself, having escaped persecution in Hungary and migrated to Australia in the 1950s following the 1956 Hungarian Revolution. Poukchanski discussed that although she did not have a background in law, law was crucial for good RRT decision making because the application of difficult provisions would ensure consistent treatment for applicants. She discussed that she found the immigration regulations 'quite complicated' and that they took 'a lot of mental power to understand'. She boasted that her first case was a fascinating one because it was so difficult and it posed an 'incredible legal dilemma which it took [her] ages to work out'. In this difficult task of utilising one's intellect to apply the law, the end goal for Poukchanski was the delivery of procedural justice through consistent treatment for the applicant:

> And I found the immigration regulations quite complicated. My very first case was a fascinating one, which all my cases were, but my very first case posed me with this incredible legal dilemma, which it took me ages to work out. The dilemma was whether someone had or hadn't applied in time within a certain period that they had to apply, otherwise their application had to be considered under a different regulation. And it was hard to work the answer out, but in the end at least it meant that if you got it right, all the applicants were treated the same.

In these narratives, the law was a foundational cornerstone of good administration: a guiding framework to be applied consistently to all but so difficult that it could only be mastered by some.

Like Poukchanski, Betty Reynolds[25] also idealised getting the difficult and reasoned law right. Despite having worked in many legal roles for government and private firms before starting on the tribunal, Reynolds did not attribute her ability to get the law right to her practical experience; she credited her intellectual ability to reason.

Whilst for Reynolds, legal training was not crucial to conducting the refugee status determination, it did tend to provide a solid basis for the provision of broader intellectual skills required to understand and apply the law. When asked to elaborate on the role that a legal background played in shaping decision making, Reynolds responded,

> You had to go back and suspend judgment and start from the first principles again and really be smart about it and build up a legal case in your mind about it all.

For Reynolds, going back to 'first principles' was associated with constructing a legal case and applying the law to arrive at a correct decision. People without a legal background generally struggled because they could not suspend judgement and return to the first principles that the law, for Reynolds, inherently recognised.

For Reynolds, as for Poukchanski and Wilson in these instances and many other interviewed participants at various points, the law was a body of logical rules or reasons derived from first principles over the ages. In this, the law was majestic and all-encompassing. Its application allowed for the greatest sense of justice to be achieved in that individuals would be treated alike through its consistent application.

You will recall Simpson – the professor of law who had extensive teaching, research, legal and travel experience and was often highly critical of the law's ability to produce rightful outcomes. In those moments, he idealised the richness that cultural awareness gained through life experience could bring to good decision making in a way that the law could not.

Recall that for Simpson, the cultural ignorance of the law was so problematic that it actually motivated his desire to be on the tribunal in the first place – he saw the tribunal as a practical forum where his rich experience could make a real difference to people's lives in a dynamic setting. In those moments, Simpson reflected that his international travel and living experience 'equipped [him] to understand' the live issues in a case. He reflected that meeting someone from Afghanistan in one moment, Somalia the next, and Mali the next – which was a common occurrence when he lived in Africa – gives one a 'rich tapestry of human connection' which means that you are 'equipped to understand'. For Simpson, such experience meant that 'you have a sense of humanity, which allows you to assess what someone is telling you' so that you can come to a truthful assessment of the applicants' claims and thus reach a fair decision. And yet at other moments in time for Simpson, the law was paramount for the analytical traits that it embodied. Simpson offered,

> To my mind it's important that they [tribunal decision makers] should have a legal background. In fact, the funny thing about having a legal background is that it equips you intellectually and perhaps even to the point of equipping you to deal with intellectual, perhaps even psychological problems also . . . It's not enough. Law is a funny business because you are taught legal rules but you also know that legal rules by themselves have got to fit properly together to get the best out of situations. Legal rules don't interpret themselves, they only guide you to make appropriate responsible decisions. And that's what I think good lawyers do.

For Simpson, although the law is not enough to guide good decision making, the analytical skills embodied in legal training are crucial for good RRT decision making. Simpson perceived the analytical skills *represented through the law* as crucial for dealing with intellectual problems that might arise in the onerous decision-making process. For Simpson, it was the law and the lawyer's 'legal mind' that allowed for a sense of balance and consistency in tribunal procedure – 'it takes a legally trained mind to make that fine distinction to say that: "we need to maintain a balance here"'. For Simpson, although the law does not equip one to access the 'rich tapestry of human connection' that broader personal experience facilitates, the letter of the law might be studied and considered in order to discern how various elements of the picture fit together and in order to interpret complex situations and thus make balanced and consistent decisions.

Another participant demonstrating the close connections between 'before-the-law' legal consciousness and a strong regard for procedural justice was Julie Henderson.[26] Henderson spoke about the immense difficulty of decision making in the RRT. This was a difficulty that she perceived derived from its complex legal parameters, which Henderson expressed in concurrence with a clear regard for the importance of information processing. Henderson was new to the law when beginning on the tribunal, having worked for many years beforehand for various government departments in non-legal, policy-focused roles. When asked to share some standout recollections of her time on the tribunal, Henderson discussed its legal difficulty and complexity, and linked this difficulty to the important and interconnected process of sorting through large amounts of law and information to discern the appropriate outcome to a claim. Henderson offered that it did not matter how good your knowledge of the legal criteria was; even if you had a good knowledge of the criteria of a 'refugee', you still needed the additional ability to understand and apply a wide range of legal rules and write a decision that can stand up in court. As Henderson said, 'the ability to write a decision that stands up in court is, I think, extremely difficult'. She recounted,

> I think it is a very complex legal framework ummm and you do – there's a certain skilled task of taking or fixing through a series of facts which may themselves be very difficult to establish anyway, and to sort of find your way through the legal framework and write a decision that's a sound decision is what's so hard.

Henderson commented that the more difficult decisions to make were those where the decision maker affirmed the decision because they were the ones that were open to appeal by the applicant. She explained that decision makers were inclined to give up on writing rigorous decisions and would instead just send them back to the department because those decisions were easier to write than decisions that could be appealed. When asked how often this practice occurred, Henderson replied that it was commonplace and that the difficulty of the law – combined with the desire for self-preservation and the need to process very large amounts of legal information – was what drove individuals to write less legally robust decisions:

> Yes, it happened a lot. The courts I would have said really overturn those decisions on the . . . and so one of the things that may have been a difficult area to work in in that legal context is that the judicial law came so thick and fast that you were constantly ummm, you know . . . the monthly training, I can't remember, but as you know you're brought up to date in new cases. But to constantly readjust your own thinking to accommodate all the latest judicial decisions um did make it a challenging thing – to be able to write

> a good decision. Um just the sheer volume of judicial decisions that came down each time, I think it was a challenge.

Henderson went on to discuss that amidst this immense challenge of learning the latest judicial decisions and constantly staying on top of the latest information in order to come to a correct decision, the truth of the applicant's situation was impossible to clarify, and therefore, it was not a crucial consideration in the decision-making process. For Henderson,

> [t]he hardest thing for me was the difficulty of writing an objective, well-founded legal decision in the circumstances when you had very little to go by and you just had to say that someone wasn't a credible witness and why.

When asked whether this was solely a legal problem or whether factual or moral difficulties also arose, Henderson responded,

> Um no, I think I viewed it as a legal difficulty in terms of making decisions and writing decisions. And certainly it is always easier to say 'yes' than it is to say 'no', whether it is in the MRT or the RRT.

In these narratives, the law involved a difficult set of principles, and mastering the law required the ability to process large amounts of information to stay on top of these difficult principles. In considering this difficulty, truth verification was not seen as an important ideal – the truth was either impossible to attain or irrelevant in making a consistent, and thus procedurally fair, decision. Instead, goals of consistent treatment for applicants were deemed important when information processing was the driving ideal. The ability to process the information and apply the law in order to come to a difficult decision was seen in these moments as the cornerstone of correct and consistent administration.

'With the law'

As was recounted in the previous chapter, for some participant officials at particular moments in time, as for some of Ewick and Silbey's participant citizens and Merry's participant's experiences with court and mediation, the law was perceived as an artificial and constructed space in which people worked to responsively achieve a range of different purposes. However, where the previous chapter discussed the way that officials sometimes demonstrated an adaptable and flexible manipulation of the law to achieve a good outcome for the applicant, there were also many times when these decision makers laterally or strategically employed the law in pursuit of their own personal agendas without regard for the substantive outcomes of the applicant.

In these moments, decision makers did not embody the traits of responsive legality. Instead, in these moments, participant bureaucrats shared Ewick and Silbey's and Merry's citizens' images of law as a game; the law was viewed as a handy tool that could be used to achieve a sense of empowerment in their own job position and at the same time protect them from being humiliated through having a decision sent back from the courts for being legally incorrect. In these moments, the hard processing of information drove narrative accounts of law as a shield, whereby individuals rejected the notion that the truth was possible to know and thus desirable to discern. Instead, they idealised the information-processing capacities of decision makers, positing that properly assessing the information and applying the law would protect their decisions from findings of jurisdictional error in judicial review and give the appearance, if not achieving the reality, of procedurally correct administration.

Reflecting this vision of law as a protective shield was Sarah Van der Ven.[27] Van der Ven had never studied law herself, was the only interviewee who had never attended university, and saw the law as an iron-clad safeguard that could protect the decision maker from being undermined through a finding of jurisdictional error. Where in some moments she was 'before the law', marvelling at its logicality and grandeur, at other moments she was 'with the law', expressing that she would routinely manipulate it for her own self-protection. Van der Ven openly discussed 'plastering' her written decisions with legal cases so that she could protect them from review by the courts. She explained that, not coming from a legal background, she had to 'get up to speed with legal rhetoric' so that she could remain competitive against other decision makers in the number of decisions that she had sent back for re-decision. She said that, as a non-legally trained member, she was always anxious to know 'the results that [we] got' and 'whether they stacked up well with members who were lawyers'. When asked about her approach to assessing refugee protection claims, she said that she would first think about which was the easiest *Refugee Convention* ground to apply to the case and then assess whether that could be fitted within the applicant's history. She discussed that she would read a number of different legal documents in this process and that it would often take a long time to find a case that could apply but that sometimes 'you could fluke it in the first two'. Van der Ven discussed that she was known amongst her friends on the tribunal as having a very low set-aside rate.

When presented with a hypothetical claim about an Afghani applicant and asked whether she would award the applicant refugee status if this were a real set of claims, Van der Ven responded,

> I think this is where there would be a difference between my decision and another member's decision. I tended to be less open to accepting claims than other members. So I would say four out of five other members would have ended up saying 'yes', but I would have been really profoundly dissatisfied about this guy's claims.

Van der Ven prided herself on her hard-line decision making, and in these moments, the law was to be unapologetically manipulated to meet the decision maker's own personal goals:

> I was known amongst my friends for being hard line and having a very low set-aside rate. But it's much harder to write a negative decision. Much

> harder. Because the other lot aren't going to get appealed in courts. The only time that you faced a legal challenge was from the applicant – so if you set aside decisions you didn't have that problem, you could get through your decisions lickety-split.

Murray Murphy[28] was another participant who spoke about law as a 'shield': as a device used to preserve and protect the decision maker from having a decision sent back from the courts. Murphy had worked in the RRT for over a decade, and many of those years were spent working in the senior role of registrar of the tribunal. He recalled that he took up the position on the tribunal because he had a solid background working in associated areas in government and felt he had much to contribute in terms of his knowledge and expertise. Murphy was actively involved in many tribunal reforms and momentous policy changes in the life of the tribunal, including having been centrally involved in the shift from randomly dividing claims between members to members specialising in assessing specific countries of origin and the division of claims accordingly. Murphy's stories about his time on the tribunal therefore shed a new light on the daily operations of the tribunal and tribunal staff attitudes from a more senior and managerial perspective. It was perhaps surprising to learn that even Murphy – with more accolade and higher standing in the tribunal hierarchy than most – spoke about the self-protective function that the law served, as members needed to understand and apply the law in their decisions to protect against review from the courts above. Murphy discussed that his initial decisions were lengthy because his legal background had taught him to cite all of the requirements of the Act and all the relevant facts and pieces of evidence that supported that reading of the Act. Murphy reflected that his experience in having previously written administrative law textbooks and guides for the tribunal meant that he understood what was required to be written; he was 'on top of the relevant information' and he was 'covered in terms of the decision'. For Murphy, there was no shame in acknowledging that

> [y]es, you had to address issues that you knew the court would be interested in if you expected a review, and in many cases you needed to check the review rate – I think you could make up to 33 per cent at one time.

Jerry Islington[29] was another participant who discussed the importance of following the correct procedure for self-protective purposes, in these moments demonstrating rule-of-law compliance absent a concern for substantive fairness: in this, he significantly departed from the tone and content of the justificatory logic of responsive legality, despite sharing a similar basic inclination towards legality. Islington had a background in foreign affairs and had worked with refugees in many different government roles, including having represented the Department of Immigration and Citizenship (DIAC) on the ground in taking postings in Moscow, Argentina, Denmark and a number of South-East Asian countries. Islington was also a refugee himself who had arrived in Australia with his parents at the age of 3, having fled political persecution in Hungary. After having retired from the tribunal, Islington began working on writing a novel reflecting 'refugee issues, which I had for a long time felt very strongly about'.

Despite this passion for refugee issues, Islington, like many others, discussed the importance of the law to tribunal decision making, not in terms of its importance for the applicant but in terms of protecting the decision maker from review by the courts. For Islington, conjuring a personal sympathy for the applicant was inappropriate to properly fulfilling one's legal duties at hand, and whilst the law would not ultimately provide the correct outcome to the case, it was a strategic tool to be applied to protect the decision maker's decision from review. Islington reflected,

> My own feeling and the feeling of lots of colleagues was yes, you had jurisdictional error in the back of your mind always, because you didn't want to have your decisions sent back. You know this, I'm sure you know this – that the Federal Court can't overturn decisions and that all they're looking for is legal error; although in some cases I know that some judges went beyond that, but quite improperly I think. Some judges seemed to have a particular sympathy, as personal sympathy, for asylum applications . . . So what we were expected to do was write our decisions on the basis of law, which was the central refugee law, and Australian case law. This was central to everything and the basis of our findings about the situation in the country, which may or may not have a determinative effect on our decision making.

Here, Islington discussed that whilst the law would not change the outcome of the decision, it was a tool to be strategically incorporated as the basis for the reasons for the decision so that courts would not send the decision back for review. In expressing his view that it was improper for judges on review to go outside the bounds of the law, Islington showed a clear regard for the legal distinction between the judicial role of judges in determining issues of law and their inability to determine issues of fact under a constitutional separation of powers.[30] And whilst the RRT decision makers were to determine the outcome in accordance with the facts, the law was a protective shield to be used to guard against the decision being sent back for review.

For Murphy, Van der Ven and Islington, as for many others at various moments, the law was a tool to protect against poor decision making. In these moments, the law could not ascertain the factual truths of the situation, but it did provide a range of provisions that functioned as an external shield to protect the decision maker's decision from being sent back for review.

In these self-protective moments, participants clearly promoted the limited virtues of repressive law that Nonet and Selznick warn against, prioritising their own image of competence for the sake of their reappointment above other considerations. Where Van der Ven openly discussed 'plastering' her written decisions with legal cases so that she could protect them from review by the courts and working hard to 'get up to speed with legal rhetoric' she reflects, as Nonet and Selznick say, not a 'malign intent' but a pragmatic manipulation of law where this may be, or be perceived to be, the only solution to protecting her own interests.

Whilst this mode of governance reflects a concern for legality and the appearance of asserting rights through its assumption that rule-of-law conformity will necessarily achieve the betterment of applicant outcomes through its correct applications, it falls short of the positive emphasis on substantive justice that is a core feature of the preferred mode of responsive legality presented in this book.

The problem with rule-of-law compliance alone, as Nonet and Selznick warn, is the potential for this mode of decision making to result in the subversion of principle for personal gain. The manipulation of law for personal self-protection means that in these moments law is a dangerous tool that is readily available to consolidate power, protect privilege and win conformity.

Bureaucratic legal consciousness and administrative justice: toward responsive governance

As these narratives reveal, public officials' orientations towards legality are variously composed of their own sets of values, administrative justice goals and unique mode of decision-making preferences. When positioned 'against the law', officials pursue discretionary decision making in prioritisation of substantive justice and the idealisation of personal experience and truth verification. When positioned 'before the law', they pursue rule application for the production of procedural justice and simultaneously idealise individual intellect and information-processing abilities. And when positioned 'with the law', they are divided between pursuing purposive outcome-driven concerns for applicants and their own pragmatic concerns – in the first case, valuing experience and truth verification for the production of substantive justice and, in the second, valuing intellect and information processing and displaying a mission-free justice orientation.

To revisit Nonet and Selznick's illuminating framework we might remember their warning that institutions are inherently tainted, sharing the limitations of the social order more broadly and serving primarily as tools for exercising dominion and subsequently favouring the 'haves' over the 'have-nots'.[31]

In this discussion, Nonet and Selznick posit that a common source of repressive law is the poverty of resources available to governing elites. For this reason, repression is a highly probable accompaniment of the formation and maintenance of political order and can occur inadvertently in the pursuit of good intentions. It is not surprising then that the officials interviewed in this study widely discussed the importance of their own flexible discretionary decision making in unity with their intentions to maintain the integrity or security of their position through projecting an *impression* of legal competence by manipulating the law, demonstrating collusion within a system of repressive law in these utterances. As Nonet and Selznick's discussion of responsive law (the legal and organisational system embroiling the ideal of responsive legality) attests, this is not to say that these individuals were motivated by an entirely wrongful selfishness – they may, in fact, have considered their own self-protection important for the sake of maintaining their role for a range of good reasons: to support a family, perhaps, or to secure one's own position to make morally correct and fair decisions for applicants in the future, although these were not motivations that were explicitly discussed. But what *was* clearly discussed within these narratives was that the officials believed that they had to manipulate the law to protect themselves from losing their position.

Nonet and Selznick specify further that repression may occur when individuals intend to optimise costs and benefits for all concerned but, lacking in time and means, instead tend to resort to repressive measures. We might note here that the officials in this study discussed the role of discretionary decision making alongside the time constraints within which they operated, reflecting more archetypically repressive decision making than in moments where procedural justice through the consistent application of law was prioritised. Recall those moments when officials would move strategically 'with the law' for their own personal protection, conscious of the material constraints within which they operated. In these self-protective moments, participants clearly promoted the limited virtues of repressive law that Nonet and Selznick warn against, prioritising their own image of competence for the sake of their reappointment above other considerations. Recall that in those moments, decision makers idealised their own information-processing capacities, positing that if they properly assessed the information and applied the law, they would protect their decisions from findings of jurisdictional error in judicial review and give the appearance, if not achieving the reality, of procedurally correct administration. We might think of Sarah Van der Ven, who revealed her materially driven motivations as she moved 'with the law', routinely manipulating it for her own self-protection. Where Van der Ven discusses using legal cases to protect her decisions from review by the courts and the use of legal language to immunise her decisions from being overturned, she therefore embodies this pragmatic manipulation of law for the protection of her own interests. The problem with this mode of governance, as Nonet and Selznick warn, is its subversion of principle for personal gain. The manipulation of law for personal self-protection means that in these moments law is a dangerous tool that is readily available to consolidate power, protect privilege and win conformity.

In place of this anarchic repressive law, which corresponds with government decision makers' 'against-the-law' rejections of legality and 'with-the-law' manipulations of legality, Nonet and Selznick outline a more advanced system of autonomous law. That procedure is at the heart of law captures a major strand in the ethos of autonomous law: the taming of repression begins with the growth of a commitment to governance by rules. Procedure, in turn, is the main visible guarantee of the consistent application of rules. In this model, law is elevated above politics, whereby in interpreting and applying the law, the decision maker is to be an objective spokesperson for historically established principles and the obedient allocator of impersonal justice.

Here we might think back, for example, to Betty Reynolds's discussion of the importance of getting the reasoned and rational law right for the purposes of removing one's own subjective values from decision making and providing consistent treatment to applicants. Or we might remember Anna Starkos, who, like Reynolds, outlined that law is paramount to good decision making because it removes the human tendency to make assumptions, and as such it is a foundational cornerstone of fair decision making.

Considering these strengths, bureaucratic valuations of procedural justice and legality might be seen as reflecting a step towards the promise of political and social stability. In discussing the importance of procedural consistency and legality, public officials, at times, transcend the limitations of self-serving repressive leadership. In these moments they take a positive step forward, embracing legality and procedural justice for its ability to provide increased governmental stability. They are less sensitive in these moments to the urgencies of leadership that characterise a poverty of power that often motivates the self-protective manipulation of law, instead striving – with a sense of responsive legality – towards consistent and fair treatment for justice system users through the application of generalised and uniform legal principles.

Notes

1 See, for example, Susan Silbey, 'After Legal Consciousness' (2005) 1 *Annual Review of Law & Social Science* 355; David Engel, 'How Does the Law Matter in the Constitution of Legal Consciousness?' in Bryant G Garth and Austin Sarat (eds), *How Does the Law Matter?* (Northwestern University Press, 1998); Marc Hertogh, 'A "European" Conception of Legal Consciousness: Rediscovering Eugene Ehrlich' (2004) 31(4) *Journal of Law and Society* 455; Dave Cowan, 'Legal Consciousness: Some Observations' (2004) 67(6) *The Modern Law Review* 928; Sally Engle Merry, *Getting Justice and Getting Even: Legal Consciousness among Working Class Americans* (The University of Chicago Press, 1990); Simon Halliday and Bronwen Morgan, 'I Fought the Law and the Law Won? Legal Consciousness and the Critical Imagination' (2013) 66 *Current Legal Problems* 1, 2; Laura Beth Nielson, 'Situating Legal Consciousness: Experiences and Attitudes of Ordinary Citizens about Law and Street Harassment' (2000) 34(4) *Law and Society Review* 1061.
2 See, for example, Hertogh, above n 1, who traces a history of legal consciousness in Europe back to the works of Eugene Ehrlich in the nineteenth century.
3 See, for example, Silbey, above n 1, who argues that legal consciousness studies have largely expired in utility to socio-legal research. For a response to this, see Halliday and Morgan, above n 1.
4 See Hertogh, above n 1; Silbey, above n 1; Halliday and Morgan, above n 1.
5 Silbey, above n 1, 326.
6 Engel, above n 1, 126.
7 Ibid 357.
8 Ibid.
9 Hertogh, above n 1, 205.
10 Ibid.
11 Engel, above n 1; Hertogh, above n 1, 205.
12 For a detailed discussion of why this approach is pursued, see Chapter 3 of this book generally.
13 Patricia Ewick and Susan Silbey, *The Common Place of Law* (The University of Chicago Press, 1998).
14 Merry, above n 2, 5.
15 Ibid.
16 Nielson, above n 1, 1058.

17 Interview with [Anonymous Participant I], (semi-structured interview) (12 December 2013).
18 Interview with [Anonymous Participant L], former Refugee Review Tribunal of Australia member (16 December 2013).
19 Interview with [Anonymous Participant W], former Refugee Review Tribunal of Australia member (22 January 2014).
20 Interview with Anonymous Participant O, former Refugee Review Tribunal of Australia member (20 December 2013).
21 Interview with [Anonymous Participant T], (semi-structured interview) (13 January 2014).
22 Ewick and Silbey, above n 13, 47.
23 Interview with [Anonymous Participant R], former Refugee Review Tribunal of Australia member (10 January 2014).
24 Interview with [Anonymous Participant P], former Refugee Review Tribunal of Australia member (20 December 2013).
25 Interview with [Anonymous Participant F], former Refugee Review Tribunal of Australia member (10 December 2013).
26 Interview with [Anonymous Participant Q], former Refugee Review Tribunal of Australia member (20 December 2013).
27 Interview with [Anonymous Participant H], (semi-structured interview) (11 December 2013).
28 Interview with [Anonymous Participant V], former Refugee Review Tribunal of Australia member (16 January 2014).
29 Interview with [Anonymous Participant S], (semi-structured interview) (10 January 2014).
30 Refer to Chapter 3 of this book.
31 See Philippe Nonet and Philip Selznick, *Law and Society in Transition: Toward Responsive Law* (Harper, 1978) 79–80, xi.

Reference list

Books/articles/reports

Cowan, Dave, 'Legal Consciousness: Some Observations' (2004) 67(6) *The Modern Law Review* 928

Engel, David, 'How Does the Law Matter in the Constitution of Legal Consciousness?' in Bryant G Garth and Austin Sarat (eds), *How Does the Law Matter?* (Northwestern University Press, 1998)

Ewick, Patricia and Susan Silbey, *The Common Place of Law* (The University of Chicago Press, 1998)

Halliday, Simom and Bronwen Morgan, 'I Fought the Law and the Law Won? Legal Consciousness and the Critical Imagination' (2013) 66 *Current Legal Problems* 1, 2

Hertogh, Marc, 'A "European" Conception of Legal Consciousness: Rediscovering Eugene Ehrlich' (2004) 31(4) *Journal of Law and Society* 455

Merry, Sally Engle, *Getting Justice and Getting Even: Legal Consciousness Among Working Class Americans* (The University of Chicago Press, 1990)

Nielson, Laura Beth, 'Situating Legal Consciousness: Experiences and Attitudes of Ordinary Citizens about Law and Street Harassment' (2000) 34(4) *Law and Society Review* 1061

Nonet, Phillip and Philip Selznick, *Law and Society in Transition: Toward Responsive Law* (Harper, 1978) 79–80, xi

Silbey, Susan, 'After Legal Consciousness' (2005) 1 *Annual Review of Law & Social Science* 355

Other

Interview with [Anonymous Participant F], former Refugee Review Tribunal of Australia member (10 December 2013)
Interview with [Anonymous Participant H], (semi-structured interview) (11 December 2013)
Interview with [Anonymous Participant I], (semi-structured interview) (12 December 2013)
Interview with [Anonymous Participant L], former Refugee Review Tribunal of Australia member (16 December 2013)
Interview with [Anonymous Participant O], former Refugee Review Tribunal of Australia member (20 December 2013)
Interview with [Anonymous Participant P], former Refugee Review Tribunal of Australia member (20 December 2013)
Interview with [Anonymous Participant Q], former Refugee Review Tribunal of Australia member (20 December 2013)
Interview with [Anonymous Participant R], former Refugee Review Tribunal of Australia member (10 January 2014)
Interview with [Anonymous Participant S], (semi-structured interview) (10 January 2014)
Interview with [Anonymous Participant T], (semi-structured interview) (13 January 2014)
Interview with [Anonymous Participant V], former Refugee Review Tribunal of Australia member (16 January 2014)
Interview with [Anonymous Participant W], former Refugee Review Tribunal of Australia member (22 January 2014)

7 Final remarks

Responsive legality in good governance

Introduction

When we take a step back and apply a bird's-eye view to the studies and stories considered in this book, the overwhelming message is clear and simple but important and surprisingly new: public governance is better when its officials authentically and altruistically care about the citizens they serve and are simultaneously technically trained and competent in the rules and procedures that they are mandated to apply. Whilst governing with a combination of sensitivity and technical competence is no simple task, especially when the range of competing interests and technical complications such as those considered in the case studies in this book are at play, the broad values espoused in the responsive-legality type provide a range of features to navigate the murky tensions of governance. In this, they keep administrative action focused on achieving the best interests of citizens.

Whether in arranging organisational codes and procedures through chit-chat in Finnish saunas, processing refugee applications in Australian tribunal decision making, allocating public housing in low socio-economic Dutch neighbourhoods, respecting citizens' rights in the Japanese automobile industry or blending national and procedural rule compliance with education users' needs and concerns in global university administration, responsive legality embodies a range of positive features for twenty-first-century governance.

Co-existing features for twenty-first-century governance

In considering the elements of good twenty-first-century governance we should remember that a number of features must be present simultaneously for this emotionally aware and technically competent form of governance to be achieved.

We should recall that officials positively justifying their decisions on the basis of this type are driven by valuations of responsiveness, reflect a dual concern for substantive and procedural justice, value experiential knowledge and truth verification abilities and work to implement the rule of law, all the while moving strategically 'with the law' rather than perilously 'against the law' or purposelessly 'before the law' and in these moments demonstrating an underlying ethic of care for the applicant.

Of course, the range of normative logics captured in responsive legality does not singularly typify one decision maker or one organisation. Individuals and organisations move between the different normative logics at different moments in time – as the ideal-typical framework acknowledges. Public officials and government organisations reflect varying levels of responsive legality in association with the extent to which they feel that they are equipped with material resources to move into the 'highest' phase of decision making. Decision makers particularly show strong evidence of justifying their decisions on the basis of bureaucratic rationality when they are concerned for their own job security and wish to give the impression of competence in order to protect their position. On the other hand, they justify their decisions on the basis of responsive legality when they are secure in their position and truly confident in their own competence.

Apart from merely acknowledging its existence, we should also actively celebrate those moments when officials employ responsive legality. The internal logics of its blend of ethical concerns are compelling for a number of explored reasons, including that procedural and substantive justice are two important component features of 'justice'; information processing and explicit knowledge pursuance cannot reach the depth of understanding and factual truthfulness that the tacit pursuit of experiential knowledge that characterises the responsive-legality type provides; and the pursuit of responsive law, made possible through a normative orientation towards the master ideal of responsive legality, can logically circumvent the perils and pitfalls of anarchic, repressive governance.

In providing illustrations of these generalised movements in public administration discernible in the wider interdisciplinary literature, the government officials studied in this book have shared their complex normative positions, revealing rich and multifaceted accounts of the combination of pragmatic, procedural and substantive concerns that motivate their decision making. These narratives reveal the admirable ideologies of these responsive officials and the less admirable moments when personal self-protection minimises the officials' mission orientation and recasts them as no more than an efficient technocrat characteristic of Weber's modernist bureaucracy. To revisit the words of one of the officials,

> There are a range of elements to fair decision making that is not just about how to apply the law. In the narrow sense, applying the law is all about being a fair decision maker, so many non-legal members were very, very good members because they weren't constrained by technical legal aspects but they were just fair, decent human beings with some life experience who were able to effectively interact with the claimant and hear them fairly and come to a reasonable decision about what the claims were.[1]

And it is these moments when public officials manage to juggle many competing normative and legal concerns at once that they embody the features of responsive legality that we might celebrate. Responsive legality accounts for those times when public officials are secure in their material position and mental capabilities and transcend the need to regurgitate precedent or to information binge, it accounts for those times when they are driven by a service ethic of care and exercise the conjoined ability to respect the contours of the law and the needs of the applicant and it captures the officials' normative valuation of procedural consistency to provide like treatment for like applicants whilst tacitly appreciating the importance of pursuing substantive justice through following purposive pursuits that the malleable margins of the law allow.

The empirical dimensions of this book corroborate the critique of twentieth-century bureaucratic rationality and have provided further consideration of the causal factors that press officials to justify their decisions according to the minimal logic of this modernist model. It has also clearly corroborated Mashaw's finding that where public officials continue to justify their decisions on the basis of bureaucratic rationality, they do so valuing their own information-processing abilities. They believe in their cognitive skills, devoid of a specific consideration of the social context in which their decision is being made and in problematic disregard for the factual nuances of the claim at hand. In these moments, officials' belief in themselves is large, though there is a worrying lack of reflection on the goals or outcomes that they hope to achieve in making their decision and the mechanisms that they employ in this process. They view themselves as intellectually capable, but to what end? They are able to process large amounts of information, but for whose gain? The answer, it seems, as explored in Chapter 6, is for their own. The law is a tool to protect their decision from being overturned on review: it is a tool used to reaffirm their own competence rather than a necessary reflection that they actually are. Recurrent discussions revealed the self-motivated leanings of this legality idealising modus operandi where the application of law was not perceived as *a feature of* good decision making; it *was the extent of* good decision making. If one could 'apply the same rigid legal rules to everyone'[2] one was making a good decision, 'no matter what the outcome was'.[3] In these moments, prioritisations of justice are not *entirely missing* from bureaucratic accounts of legality, but they are *subsumed* within them. In this view, the most justice that can be done is that afforded by the routinised application prescribed by the rules of the legal system *because of* the way that they developed and the self-protection that they afforded, regardless of the substantive effect that they have on the overall outcome for the applicant.

On the other hand, public officials – sometimes the very same individuals who at other moments lack this moral competence – at different times reflect the distinctive hallmarks of higher-level leadership. They demonstrate this competence at moments when their broader life experience and desire to verify the truth drives their decision making. In prioritising their own experience and truth verification abilities, they do not deem these things important because they reflect an inherent greatness about themselves: experience is not important because it demonstrates that they are cultured, worldly or wise; truth verification abilities are not important because they demonstrate that they are perceptive, intuitive or discerning. They are considered important because they are skills that are required to bridge the divide between the technical legal regime and the sociological complexity of the environment in which their decisions are made in the interests of producing fair outcomes for applicants. Public officials must have life experience to know how to talk to an applicant, how to ask them questions, how to get to the bottom of their story. They must have truth-verifying abilities so that the decision they make honours the needs of the applicant in front of them and makes a fair assessment of their entitlements.

The procedural law is not irrelevant in this process, but it is also no more than that: it is no more than a technical process to be followed. Much more than this is needed for a decision to be a competent one. Where the information-idealising official strives to appear competent, it is in those moments of experience and truth verification idealisation that they actually are. Their responsive emphasis on applicant outcomes shows a concern for applicant welfare that is a distinctive feature of mission orientation in competent leadership. Justice is not something that can be guaranteed in a technical process alone; it is something that requires individual solutions in individual cases to produce substantively fair outcomes. As this book has argued, in the ideal-typical sense, it is in these 'with-the-law' images of legality, corresponding with idealisations of experience and truth verification for the production of substantive justice, that an admirable range of competencies and logics are employed.

In embracing responsive legality we might gradually be cured of the limitations of bureaucratic 'rationality'; and in embracing responsive legality we might continue to hope for, and see, value-rich public administration that best serves the interests of citizens and applicants in twenty-first-century governance.

Notes

1 Interview with [Anonymous Participant W], (semi-structured interview) (16 January 2014).
2 See Chapter 5.
3 Ibid.

Reference list

Other

Interview with [Anonymous Participant W], (semi-structured interview) (16 January 2014)

Index

Note: Page numbers in **bold** indicate a table on the corresponding page.

Kolibri 360 GmbH
Ferdinand-Jühlke-Straße 7
99095 Erfurt, Deutschland
produktsicherheit@kolibri360.de